UNDER MY SKIN

Drama, Trauma & Rock 'n' Roll

First Kumi Books edition 2022

Copyright ©2022 by Elise Krentzel
ALL RIGHTS RESERVED

For information about permission to reproduce selections from this book, write to info@undermyskinbook.com or to Permissions, Kumi Books LLC, 4600 Mueller Blvd. Ste. 4007, Austin, Texas 78723.

www.elisekrentzel.com

Library of Congress Cataloging-in-Publication Data
Library of Congress Control Number: 2021919218
Krentzel, Elise
Under My Skin/Elise Krentzel
P. cm.
   1. Non-Fiction   2. Biography

ISBN Paperback: 978-1-7373638-0-4
ISBN Hardcover: 978-1-7373638-2-8
ISBN Ebook: 978-1-7373638-1-1

Text set in Playfair Display
Designed by Stefan Silvestri
Formatting by Kingfisher Design

Printed in the United States of America

Dedicated to my son,
whose gentle soul, unconditional love, dry wit, and sharp intellect kept me going through the rough patches and showed me how to reclaim my true self.

Under My Skin will transport you to a different time in our culture, when rules seemed made for the breaking and an open heart, an untamed spirit, and sheer determination could take you safely to the other side of the world and back. A mind-blowing read about a young girl's journey through adolescence and the rock 'n' roll world of the 1970s.

—**Marli Higa,** Research and Copy Chief, Women's Health Magazine

The 1970s music scene in Japan was a hotbed for experimentation. We couldn't get enough Western bands from the UK and USA. Elise was at the forefront of this scene, a trendsetter and fearless young woman who forged ahead, despite her age, gender and the cultural barriers she struggled with. This book is for anyone who grew up then and for those who wish they were there.

-**Yuki Watanabe,** CEO of YWA Music & Former Owner of Mars nightclub

As a musician and NYC club owner, I spent my life hobnobbing with celebrities and rockers—KISS, Aerosmith, Peter Frampton, Guns N' Roses, Bon Jovi, and more. Elise's story brings alive the mayhem and wonder of the music scene, as seen through the eyes of a spunky, vibrant young girl finding her way through the maze of the rock 'n' roll world of the 1970s. A fascinating must-read.

—**Nicki Camp**

UNDER MY SKIN

Drama, Trauma & Rock 'n' Roll

Elise Krentzel

Kumi Books

Austin, Texas

Table of Contents

Foreword 1

Chapter 1: The Glamercy 5

Chapter 2: Fear and Helplessness 11

Chapter 3: A Recipe for Rage 21

Chapter 4: Lies, Alienation, and Creativity 35

Chapter 5: My Sexual Revolution 53

Chapter 6: Fucking My Way Through Europe 65

Chapter 7: A Nazi Son's Revenge 97

Chapter 8: I'm Gonna Be a Rock 'n' Roll Journalist 107

Chapter 9: KISS Japan Tour 1977 117

Chapter 10: A Night With the Yakuza 139

Chapter 11: Trouble in Paradise 155

Chapter 12: Bigger Than the Beatles 161

Chapter 13: Landing the Deal 173

Epilogue: The Bamboozler 177

Acknowledgments 187

About the Author 189

Foreword

The lioness inside me roared with resentment and betrayal. "If you can't say whatever lies you're spreading behind my back to my face, then walk away. You are no longer my friend," I stated, in no uncertain terms. The four or five clique girls were astonished by my brazen words. Then and there, no amount of neediness—and boy, there was no limit to that interminable longing—could deter me from standing up for myself. Even at the risk of losing that "friend."

Perhaps it was the conviction to dig out the truth and let the light of day shine on it. I needed confrontation. I faced any consequences head-on. I wished others would do the same.

That became a running theme in my life: facing the truth! I'd strayed so far from my path that it took nearly five decades to confront my constant need for acceptance—from an intimate partner, parents, friends, and extended family. One by one, my nuclear family died; partnerships faded into the distance. I became self-liberated.

Shakespeare would've been proud of the people in my life for their characteristics—humanity's worst in class. Until I was a teenager, Mom was physically and emotionally abusive. Dad, on the other hand, never raised a hand against us yet was proud of his small-time con games. My stepfather dealt pills on the side; eventually my brother became a heroin addict. Adding to this desperate cast of lowlifes, I inherited an über-materialistic stepmother with significant control issues who regularly burst into hysterical screaming rants. Was she a doppelgänger of my mother in the emotional sense? If something didn't go her way, she became rabid.

An insufferable union was just the prelude to the icing on Elise Krentzel's cake. Husband number one was Japanese; he betrayed me, then tried to ruin my reputation. Number two, from Switzerland, should have been my business partner exclusively, as we had a director-producer relationship: like-minded intellectually and creatively, yet emotionally empty. There were holes in that marriage—a case of the great Swiss cheese meltdown. Number three was Dutch and eleven years younger, the father of my only child. I wasted precious years trying to "reform" him: He was a great disappointment in the areas of empathy, self-awareness, and polite mannerisms. Our divorce almost cost me custody of my son and forced me into financial ruin.

Yet from all these intense sufferings I learned grace and humility, and how much these qualities fortified my soul. When I was forty-four, the birth of my son helped restore a deeply buried yet unsullied ability to love completely and unconditionally. I thought my mother was my harshest critic, but I discovered I'd taken it up a few notches without her help. Finally, the love I'd been searching for outside myself was earned by looking within, excavating those demonic parts I'd attributed to others but discovered painfully were mine all along. In other words, I became a whole human being and graduated with a Ph.D. in Life.

I am genuinely grateful to my deceased parents and brother, all my exes, and the extended families for playing a crucial part

Foreword

in my life's dramas, because they performed pivotal roles in my development. If it weren't for them, I wouldn't be the person I am today.

I used to be a drama queen, but now I'm just a queen.

Chapter 1 – The Glamercy

New York City 1984

After I returned from Japan, I lived with my friend Paul in the city. I sometimes stayed over at my mother and stepfather's bayside high-rise condo in, um, Bayside, Queens (authentic original branding!), as they'd sold the house in Dix Hills. I'd meet Mom about twice a month in the city, usually on a Friday for happy hour. We planned to meet at the legendary rock 'n' roll bar at the Gramercy Hotel on a Friday (known as the "Glamercy" since 1973, when David Bowie stayed there for a couple of weeks on his U.S. tour). Mom invited me to sleep over for the weekend. The plan was to drive back to Bayside.

That day I had a raucous time with my buddy Laraine Newman, of *SNL* fame. We smoked a joint at Paul's apartment, then headed over to H&H Bagels (best in the city if not the world) to share an everything bagel with schmear.

Walking down Broadway, we laughed while munching. We made fun of the many weird-looking strangers on the street: a gal with mottled Rastafarian hair who only wore a dirty bikini with tassels while riding a bicycle, or the overweight drag queen whose makeup was smeared up past her eyebrows. We were a bit tired, so we took the subway one stop to another infamous rock 'n' roll hotel on the Upper West Side, the Empire. We arrived ahead of Laraine's crew and plunked ourselves down at a long table that seated twelve, overlooking Central Park West. As they filed in, I noticed a hunk named Jerry, a grip on the show. The rest of the afternoon was spent kibitzing around and imbibing champagne.

Jerry sat down next to me because I was not too subtle about my interest in him, grinning that big Cheshire cat smile of mine. His Bloody Mary arrived, and I almost tipped it over with my elbow. He caught it just in time.

"Slow down, little lady!" he said, startled, yet his agreeable flirting was drawing me in. I did not heed his warning. His doe eyes beckoned me. Without his explicit permission, I sat on his lap, running my hands through his thick, wavy chocolate hair. We talked about what he did on the show, bands we liked, concerts we'd been to. I told him about some of my memorable Japan experiences. The day got away from me; soon it was time to meet Mom and my stepdad Mike downtown. Jerry and I exchanged numbers; we decided to meet up the following weekend at the *SNL* studio after work.

At the Glamercy, I sat in the booth nearest the door to wait for my parents. I ordered my go-to cocktail, a Blue Lagoon. After years of drinking only beer, sake, shochu, and whiskey in Japan, I delighted in mixed cocktails again!

Just as the drink was served, Mom and Mike made a wobbly entrance. Before she sat down, I felt Mom was priming herself for an argument. The air was thick with trepidation. Mike ordered drinks for the two of them while I waited for some kind of an outburst; my heart was beating wildly, a familiar feeling I dreaded and had always expertly suppressed through cajoling or humor, or by ignoring them.

Chapter 1 - The Glamercy

As soon as she had the Stoli on ice with a twist in her hand, an argument ensued. "You shouldn't have come home from Japan, Elise, 'cause you're just a burden on us," she stammered. Mike nodded in agreement, looking at my mother as if they were two druggies in on some secret.

I looked at both of them incredulously. I felt dejected. For a split second, I was speechless. How could a mother say this to her dutiful daughter? I did everything she ever asked of me. I essentially raised my little brother, Richard; I comforted her whenever she went berserk, which was practically all the time; I cleaned, cooked, and took care of my stuff. Despite my protestations over her marrying Mike, I still showed him respect and consideration. What else did she want from me? And him—who the hell did he think he was, coming between my mother and me? He probably influenced her in a drugged-out state of mind.

I let out an uninhibited, wolf-like howl. I didn't care if everyone at the bar heard me. "How could you be so callous to say that? I've never been a burden to you or Mike. Richard is the one who's the burden—he's the drug addict living at home with you, mooching off you."

"You've always got an answer, don't you, wiseass. I'll give you something to answer!" Just as she was about to swing her arm, Mike grabbed it and told her to shut the fuck up. The servers were smart enough not to come close to our table. The ice was melting into our drinks; I hoped that would dilute the explosiveness of the situation.

At that point, I had no clue about either of her two diseases. Drinking enraged her bipolar self, turning her into a mean, bad drunk, the kind portrayed in films like the flick *Barfly*. She sprang up from her chair, yelling, "Pay the bill! I want to leave. Right now." My stepdad acquiesced without turning toward me. The Sex Pistols' "God Save the Queen" hammered through the PA system, and I thought, "Me, that's about me."

I tried reasoning with Mike. He ignored me. I pleaded with the madwoman to sit down, which never works, but stubborn optimist that I was, I begged.

"Mom, please don't do this. Wait, Mom, let's talk this out; there's no reason to leave. *Moooooommmm*, listen to me!" My heart sped up as it used to when I was growing up in the insane asylum called "home" and had no grasp of her medical condition. Had I known she was suffering from alcoholism or a coke addiction, I would've tried to save her, though I probably would have failed just as I had with my brother.

My pleas for her to stop fell on deaf ears. She stormed out of the bar, muttering curses, flailing her arms, making a scene, while I followed. Mike, familiar with this routine and a co-conspirator, waved the valet to get the car. He gave the guy a crumpled bunch of dollar bills for his discretion. I watched the black Cadillac speed away as I stood there in a pool of tears, unable to move a muscle.

There were no cell phones, only public payphones at that time. It would take a good forty-five minutes for my Mom and stepdad to drive back to Bayside. It was cold and dark. I couldn't stand there...but what could I do? Hitchhike to Queens? Freeze to death? God only knew! I had no money, just my little overnight bag for the weekend. I'd spent all but a few quarters during the

Chapter 1 - The Glamercy

day at the Empire. Frantically, I paged through my handwritten entries in the pocket-sized phone book I kept in my fringed bag and called Jerry collect. He accepted the call.

Shivering, I admitted, "Jerry, I'm so sorry I called collect. My mother just threw me out on the street and drove off without leaving me a penny."

"What the hell?" He was surprised. "Where are you calling me from?"

"I'm at the Glamercy. I need a place to spend the night and also some train fare for tomorrow to get back home...."

"That's not cool, man. Come on over. We'll talk about it. My address is 560 West 49th in Hell's Kitchen. Do you have any money for a bus?" he asked.

"Nothing at all. I spent it this afternoon, and as I said, my mother just took off in the car; she lives in Bayside. Lemme go now, or else I'll freeze. I'll just walk fast."

"OK, I'm here. Just ring the buzzer when you arrive. I'll be ready with a towel."

I walked more than forty blocks in that horrid weather to get to Jerry's apartment. After slugging up four flights of stairs to his tenement flat, I rang his doorbell. Before I could say my name, the door opened. Jerry handed me a warm towel. A hot bath and two glasses of red wine waited for me (and him).

Chapter 2 – Fear and Helplessness

The Bronx, NYC 1961

My family was culturally Jewish on both sides and somewhat religious. My maternal grandfather emigrated as a teenager with his parents and sisters from Austria, and my grandmother emigrated from Germany just in time to escape the onslaught of crimes against Jewish citizens pre-Holocaust. They were faux Conservatives, kept a Kosher home, and celebrated the Sabbath and the big three holidays, yet didn't attend synagogue except on urgent business. Dad's parents were from adjacent towns in Belarus—Minsk and Pinsk—but they were no Laurel and Hardy. They joined in at family gatherings and spoke less Yiddish than my other grandparents.

My parents were what you call "reform secular Jews," meaning they were born into the faith yet didn't practice it. Like many of that generation in the 1950s, my parents rebelled by doing the polar opposite of what their parents taught.

After three weeks of riding Duke Ellington's A train to the city for work, my parents' initial encounter on the subway went lustful. They decided to elope to escape the confines of their parents' environment and oppressive rules, much to the consternation of both of their parents, though for different reasons. Mom's mother, Faye, wanted her daughter to have a traditional Jewish wedding. Lily, Dad's mom, was more perturbed about the loss of a caretaker for her other son, who was disabled.

Dad's dad, Grandpa Mershey (we used to make fun of him—"Grandpa Mershey the Hershey bar"), was a man of few words and many smiles. His impressive hands were always black around the nails from handling the vegetables, fruits, and nuts at his greengrocer's shop. He worked twelve-hour days, six days a week, to provide the amenities of a working-class lifestyle. My father was made responsible for his younger brother.

Grandma would shout at him from the kitchen window adjacent to the fire escape. "Make sure you're taking care of your brother, Yonkel. Don't stay out late with your friends or you'll get it handed to you," she yelled as she slammed the window shut and locked it by flipping the two levers on top. Off to work as a waitress she went, leaving little Yonkel (Jack) in despair. As a latchkey kid, Dad was tasked with the unbearable and impossible responsibility of watching out for his younger brother Sid, who had epilepsy, after school until Grandma returned home.

How could my grandmother make her son responsible for taking care of another child who had a disease that was scorned and ridiculed in society? Besides, Dad knew that if Sid had a seizure and a pencil couldn't be found to put in his mouth in time, he might die, and my father would be blamed. Caught between a rock and a hard place, Jack turned his attention toward entertaining his friends with his sharp wit and pranks.

Grandma Faye demanded that my Mom date only Jewish boys in their all-Italian neighborhood. That, of course, was a ridiculous and nearly impossible task. There were hardly any Jewish boys in Mom's school, if any at all. She was a tomboy (and quite the wild one). She dated the drummer from the famous 1950s–'60s band, the Four Seasons. He wasn't Jewish! When Grandma Lilh found out, she belted Mom with her strong hands. Faye was a screamer to offset Grandpa Irving's reserved demeanor, which is probably where Mom got her training in lung development.

The Bronx, NYC, November 22, 1955

Mom was eighteen, and Dad, twenty-two. They celebrated their wedding dinner at the prix fixe Italian restaurant Marchi's in Manhattan. That same year, Mom got pregnant and, eight months later, gave birth to twins—a boy and a girl who died prematurely at three weeks old. In 1956 there was no technology to save those tiny souls (nor, did it seem, was there any empathy for the parents!).

Without a breath to process the grief and heartbreak of their loss, and upon doctor's orders, my parents hastily made hay while the tears dropped. I was born under two stars, the death and horse star, in 1957. Two years later, my baby brother Richard was born under the stars of abandonment and anger.

When I was five years old, Dad disappeared. I was disconsolate because all Mom could do was flop herself down on the sofa like a rag doll and cry all day. I missed Dad's greetings when he came home from work. Every night before dinner he'd run up to me first because I was older, with a big smile and warm hugs that graduated to tickling and finally ended in hysterics, with me pleading, "Let me go, Daddy! Stop it! Stop it!"

Mom said he had a business trip (whatever that meant)

Under My Skin

to Buffalo, New York, a faraway place. It was all the way north near the majestic Niagara Falls. I sat at the foot of our leaf green Bergère chair in the living room, caressing Mom's knees, trying to grab all her misery in my small arms. She was crumpled into a ball, wailing at the top of her lungs. For a disquieting moment, I imagined Daddy falling off the falls, tumbling to the bottom, broken, never to return to us.

I was able to calm her down, the way children do, with real caresses and deep empathy. I reminded her softly that Richard, Grandma Faye, Grandpa Irving, and I loved her, that Daddy would return and everything would be all right. Her sadness would be for naught.

As her grief subsided, I must have fallen asleep from exhaustion right there on the floor. When I woke up from a nightmare the following morning in my bed, I was crying at the top of my lungs, "Daddy, Daddy, where are you?"

Folklore in our family was passed down from one guilty generation to the next through stories of woe, anguish, suffering, and the nasty things perpetrated on the victim telling the tale. I have no recollection of being rushed to the hospital, but Mom told the story enough times for the imprint to seem like a reasonable facsimile of the truth.

"Why did the child tiptoe to the medicine cabinet?" Dad joked.

I walked into the bathroom, and for a moment, my bare feet tingled on the black-and-white hexagonal-tiled floor. I climbed up on the porcelain toilet seat to the sink and leaned precariously over it. I jammed open the lead glass cabinet and grabbed the

Chapter 2 - Fear and Helplessness

bottle of St. Joseph Aspirin for Children from the top shelf. They were pink. I chewed them all.

I don't recall what time of day it was when I downed those puppies, but Mom discovered my thin, long body tangled on the floor of the one bathroom we all shared. She called an emergency ambulance that came to whisk us away. My Dad was still on a "business trip." Grandma Faye arrived later, once I was able to see and talk again. Grandpa Irving was a medallion taxi driver and worked twelve-hour shifts, so he couldn't make it. My little brother was so cuddly; he jumped up on the hospital bed to give me kisses, as did Grandma Faye. Mom squeezed my hand and pecked my cheek but was so distraught that all she did was pace the room and chain-smoke. Grandma bellowed, "Sit down already, would ya? Stop pacing. You're making me nervous."

From that early age and for a long time afterward, I believed something was inherently wrong with me, which set me apart and made me deficient. To be on par with others, I felt I needed to compensate and prove my worth. By giving all my love—and I do mean one hundred percent of it—to save my parents from their infirmities, the person I should have become vanished.

I was going to fix my family because I could. I knew I could since I had this incredible ability to see through people as if my eyes were laser guns. I knew at that tender age that since I could detect who was lying, phony, or insincere, and pinpoint someone's melancholy or joy, I could make them feel better. Dad didn't come home for another couple of weeks, so I had to find a way to keep my parents together and happy.

Mom constantly slapped me on my face or my tushy, and I

had to protect my brother from her rants and rages. They'd come out of the clear blue sky or the dark gray clouds. I never knew when she'd attack with her screeches or her hands. After slapping me she'd lose steam and hug me, then look at my red face and speak words of tenderness: "My little Lisey, you're so precious"; and all I'd do was cry, cry, cry. My intuitive radar had no shield or veil. I disarmed people with my penetrating eyes that sought a connection to their innermost soul. But not Mom's. She only allowed me to see a sliver of the love inside after I yelped.

My one friend, Laurie, older by two years, understood my sensitivities. She never once crossed my line of trust, unlike the adults in my life. Her silent and total acceptance of me was unmatched except by one other person: Grandma Faye. Both of them loved me unconditionally. I guess my brother did too, but I didn't count him since he was too young to verbalize anything. *And* I was secretly jealous.

Each time Mom, Richard, and I strolled down the Grand Concourse or in the city, everyone—literally every passerby—would stop in wonderment and exclaim, "What a gorgeous baby!" and "He's so beautiful!" leaving me in the lurch. Mom never once took a look at me during these peacock sessions. She didn't flatter me. Why would she? Appearances are what mattered to her, not real feelings.

I would chime in something bright to gain attention. The only way to be noticed was to use my personality since I believed I was ugly. I didn't get any reinforcement from my mother saying what a cute or beautiful child I was. My smart remarks and witticisms gained some attention and elicited comments or giggles

Chapter 2 - Fear and Helplessness

from strangers, but it wasn't the same as being complimented for your looks. Wit and intellect took second place to appearances. My brother didn't have to raise a finger or do anything unique to get compliments. That boiled my blood and set in motion a lifelong pattern of overdoing and overachieving to gain attention, whether in the public eye or privately in my intimate relationships.

I had to work for the morsels of attention I earned. There was no resting or taking it easy for me. Life was a struggle; to be noticed, cherished, and admired meant I had to work ten times harder than anyone else around me.

Mom quite aggressively shut down my talent of seeing through people. She didn't want, nor could she allow herself, to be exposed in front of me. The only time I was permitted to show the depth of my feelings was when Mother Freeloader needed my sweet, tender love. She was an emotional vampire. She must have read Dogen, a thirteenth-century Japanese Buddhist teacher who said, "We must always be disturbed by the truth."

It would take me decades to accept my innate ability to see with clarity the essence of people not as a liability, but as a superpower. A rock star's superpower. One that could protect me from predators and evildoers; one that, had I trusted myself, could have protected me from my own parents. A superpower that, when turned inward, could reveal all the precious gems inside my soul.

Dad shut this ability down too—in me and in himself. He masked his gloom and double life with incessant humor. If I was crying, Dad was the parent to caress and hold me. The moment I stopped, he'd tickle me until I was crying with laughter. Yet that hysterical laughter soon mutated to a hidden rage, as he wouldn't let up until I was either panting for breath or yelling with pent-up frustration.

During the time Dad was away, a friend of Mom's—a man—came to visit her. He would seduce me with candy and other treats while Mom was busy preparing lunch or dinner in the kitchen. I would sit on his lap, and he'd rock his leg back and forth. It felt like a game of choo-choo train. Only it wasn't! He was getting a hard-on and rubbing my underwear under my skirt. I didn't understand what was happening, but he held me tight and whispered in my ear, "Never tell your mother about this, or else you'll be in big trouble."

I told Mom what was happening with her friend because I couldn't tell a lie, even if I promised him I wouldn't say a word. I didn't like the game he was playing after a few times. It felt yucky. Wrong. "Mom, your friend puts me on his lap when you're not looking. He touches me, Mom, by my vagina on my panties."

I knew what a vagina and a penis were. My parents were home educators in some things, like the human body. Dad walked around nude, as did Mom sometimes. It was the sixties and Mom was a hippie, mentally and artistically. Dad was just weird.

Instead of believing me, she screamed her head off: "You're lying to me. Tell me the truth!" She shook me until I almost fainted. I ran to my room to weep into my pillow. Since I shared the room with my brother, he buried himself in his play to avoid the confrontations.

I must have taken those pretty pink pills sometime after I

Chapter 2 - Fear and Helplessness

told my mother about that man and before my father returned home.

Eventually, when my father did return, it was against my mother's will. She'd found one of his white uniform shirts from the beauty salon in the hamper, reeking of White Shoulders perfume. She begged Grandma Faye to take us all in; Grandma flat-out refused. According to Jewish law, it was a crime to get a Git (divorce). The statutes of Gittin only provided for a divorce initiated by the husband.

Grandma would never allow Mom to leave her husband. Mom had to bear the brunt of her husband's infidelity and just suck it up. Knowing she was living with a sex addict clouded their marriage and our lives with a slow brew of malcontent, which led to full-blown mistrust and resentment. Mom found a boyfriend herself as a matter of principle and vengefulness.

My Dad was larger than life to me, his little Lisey. When he finally returned weeks later, he strolled into the house in his jovial manner with a Santa Claus sachet of toys for my baby brother and me. I recall a Mickey Mouse watch, a lot of games, and a Barbie suitcase filled with Barbie, Ken, and Midge with tons of outfits. Richard got some rubbery toys like Gumby and Pokey, model airplanes, and my brother's first Lionel train set. There was a plastic Mothra, which I smashed by jumping up and down on it until it shattered into pieces. Mom slapped the living daylights out of me for breaking his toy.

I had no out. No outlet. I disappeared into myself like a Matryoshka doll. There was no way to express the crimes committed against my little person. Yet I still loved; I knew I did

Under My Skin

because I felt an unselfish love for everyone at the same time. Still my heart remained camouflaged. What I showed to the outside world was a plastic smile with two dots for rouged cheeks.

Chapter 3 - A Recipe for Rage

East Bronx, NYC, Late 1940s

One time during a high school lunch break, Dad was hanging out with his crowd in the East Bronx—Lowell, Stan, Lenny, and Irwin—at the concrete schoolyard out back. They schemed to take the math teacher's papers and regrade them. Maybe Jack was the mastermind behind it, but he wasn't going to be a patsy. He sent in Irwin, the least conspicuous-looking (Irwin the Bookworm, as he was nicknamed), who grabbed the papers from the unlocked room and made a dash for the back door.

He leaned on the metal bar and the papers went flying all over the place. Distraught and scared, he ran out to tell the boys what had happened, the papers still on the floor. When Jack and his friends rushed in to gather the papers, a light went on in Jack's head: I'll return these to the classroom as if nothing happened, and if I meet the teacher, I'll tell him I saw someone steal the papers. Then I'll be the good guy returning the stolen papers.

That's what he did, and sure enough, the teacher thanked him profusely and gave him a notch up on his poor grades. Dad couldn't stand school and eventually dropped out after less than a year of putting up with all the crap and rules. He was seventeen.

Kew Gardens, Queens 1962–1969

Kicking and shouting, my brother and I were uprooted and moved from the Bronx to the "better borough" of Queens. The diaspora of Jewish families—those first-gen children of immigrants like my parents—from the leafy, hilly borough to other areas within the greater New York City area, began in earnest in the sixties. I was distraught at having to leave my best friend, Laurie; the last thing I ever wanted was to move away from her. I couldn't imagine I'd ever make another friend as close. She was like an older sister to me. I was indeed left all alone.

No matter how much I demanded to have Laurie's phone number, Mom wouldn't budge. She unilaterally decided it was best to forget all about her. How cruel! After our move, no amount of protestation would bring her back. I never saw her again.

Our building, the Texas, was located on Austin Street. The area we lived in was beautiful and looked very British, with Tudor-style apartment buildings and parks everywhere. Our middle-class, square brick apartment building was one of the hundreds of post-war constructions to be found all over the five boroughs.

We lived on the third floor facing the street in a two-bedroom, two-bath with living/dining room en suite and a separate kitchen and terrace. My brother and I shared the master bedroom (just like in the Bronx), which I detested. He snored, and I couldn't sleep.

Worse, Mom made me make his bed in addition to mine because I was the more "responsible one." He could get away with anything and never get punished. But for me? Not a fat chance in

Chapter 3 - A Recipe for Rage

hell. Did I have *walk on me* written on my forehead? I struggled with wanting to please and doing good despite growing resentment toward the slacker-in-the-making my brother was becoming. The same went for setting the table at dinner. He never had to lay a fork, knife, or spoon down unless he was using it to shovel food into his mouth.

Although our nuclear unit consisted of four members, once we moved into our new digs, it felt as if we had inherited a vast amount of siblings.

The motley crew of this extended family consisted of three other core couples and their children: Lowell and Lois and their daughters, Michelle and Wendy, who were my age and my brother's age, respectively; Roz and Lefty and their son, Craig, who was four years younger than me; and Lillian and Stan and their daughter, Stephanie, who was Richard's age. The six kids were fondly called the "little rascals" by the parents. For each other, we created nasty nicknames.

Richard was called "square and round," as his ears were of two different shapes. I was "brace face" because of my ungainly braces with rubber bands that seemed to take up the entirety of my small face. Michelle and Wendy were "skinny" and "fat," respectively. Stephanie was named "Stephonic" (she loved listening to AM radio from her transistor Sony and our stereo system). Craig, well, he was just a little idiot we all adored. For sure, I was the ringleader of this band, instigating trouble at every opportunity.

The dads—Lowell, Stan, Lefty, and my father—had grown up on the same block and gone to junior high and high school together. After graduating high school, Lowell started a cosmetic supply company. Stan worked in advertising, and Lefty in the schmata trade. Dad was a badass salesman and worked from home, the original freelancer selling everything from beauty supplies and tractor trailers to real estate. He was the only high school dropout amongst his peers, without any aptitude for reading. That's why Mom was the one who read to us children. Except for album liner notes and the *TV Guide*, Dad couldn't care less—a trait my brother adopted. Despite a very small vocabulary, Dad was a master of the pun and could turn a phrase like magic. I did not take after his reading habits but did have his quick wit.

The men all seemed to marry within three years of one another. Their wives became besties after tying the knot—a big gaggle of girls. Then kids started popping out, one after the other.

The mothers seemed to take a kibbutz approach to child-rearing. They were somewhat interchangeable. It seemed to work, but only in the departments of reprimanding and sandwich-making. All the mothers yelled their heads off at us. Some pinched, some slapped, others punished us hard, until they all got bored. When they tired of supervising our little tushies, they poured themselves tall glasses of gin and tonics or sipped whiskey sours from one of their dry bars.

What became a multiple-family tradition for years on end was Sunday night dinner at the local Chinese restaurant on Queens Boulevard with Mom and Dad's best friends and the gang of rascals. They would reserve the back room for us. We were a rowdy bunch. When we children weren't running around the lazy Susan tables at the restaurant, flinging fortune cookies at each other, we were indulging in spare ribs, mixed lo mein, and shrimp in lobster sauce. Typical Cantonese shlock. I taught myself how to use those slippery plastic mah-jongg-tile-colored chopsticks before I was ten by imitating the visual instructions on the chopstick paper covering!

On other weekends, the parents organized group outings. While we didn't travel very far mileage-wise, we were invariably on the go locally, visiting the famous World's Fair, taking walks near the duck pond after shopping at Lord & Taylor's in Little Neck, or picnicking or ice skating in New Jersey. On other weekends we'd visit berry and pumpkin farms on Long Island or the zoo at Central Park. One of my favorite trips was to Mystic Seaport, Connecticut, where I took what I thought was an award-winning Instamatic photograph of my brother kneeling in the ocean with the waves crashing to shore. His countenance was in shadow against the glistening sun rays.

Another outing was to a small playhouse in Manhattan on the Upper East Side near 57th Street (I remember that because it was close to Serendipity's, where we all indulged in the best-ever ice cream sundaes, big enough for four adults to share). The parents dropped us kids off alone to see *Hansel and Gretel*. The kick was the gingerbread house onstage made of real candy, and after the show, we piled onstage to eat the house down.

Of course, we were in each other's apartments and homes. We spanned the borough of Queens. Only Lowell and Lois, with their kids Michelle and Wendy, lived in a spacious, ranch-style home in Melville on Long Island with an expensive half-acre of sloping land.

Practically every summer, at least one weekend day beginning at the end of June through Labor Day in September, was spent with the whole lot of us at Jones Beach, Field Number Five, getting tanned. On rare occasions, my first cousin Gene would join us. He was a nice boy (although a bit socially awkward), so he missed out on the fun as he preferred to be alone building sandcastles or daydreaming about becoming a marine biologist, which I thought was fancy.

My parents were still pretty irresponsible. You can't call criticism a parenting technique. Despite Mom's daily reminders—which, of course, I had engraved in my memory—of how to treat my brother, or how to speak in public (read: suppress my real thoughts), she never let up on berating me for what I wasn't doing right. Her slights were crushing. And contradictory.

"If you don't care what other people think, then why should I?"

"There's a proper way to behave toward people, Elise. You can't just say your opinions anytime the thought comes to you," she pressed.

"Why not?" I countered.

"Do you want me to slap you?"

Whenever I asked why, she'd either threaten me or just click her tongue and roll her eyes, making the *tsk* sound, then walk away or change the subject, usually to something stupid like "Do you want a tuna fish sandwich?"

I continued to mother her emotionally with the added burden of looking after my brother. My father was a goofball. The moment anything became severe, he disappeared into his role as a clown.

Chapter 3 - A Recipe for Rage

To my parents, it was more important to have fun with their friends and groove to the recordings of the Beatles, Nancy Sinatra, the Supremes, or Barbra Streisand than to be present for their children's emotional needs. On the other hand, they encouraged me to perform karaoke-style to the music played on our all-in-one TV and Panasonic stereo system.

Dad was a jazz music aficionado who collected 45s, EPs, and LPs. His collection amounted to over one thousand discs, dating from the 1930s to the late significant band jazz era of the '40s. When Mom and I were bored stiff with Dad's monotonous records, we did the Twist, the Freddie, and the Swim to rock and pop music. Mom also indulged in classical music—from Chopin to Mussorgsky, a relief from her cacophony of shrieks. Both of them loved dancing. But not together. Dad snapped his fingers while wearing his headphones. I guess we were the original Walkman type of family?

Mom was the "artistic" one. She introduced the concepts of being up-to-date in fashion, playing an instrument, interior decorating, sculpting, arts and crafts, and the performing arts, especially classical ballet. At one point, she gave me a choice between guitar and ballet lessons. I chose the former.

I loved singing and dancing as much as playing the guitar. I tried teaching my brother to dance, but he had two left feet and didn't seem too interested. He chose electric guitar because, hey, he was a boy and wanted to blast the music on his kid-sized amp. I had the talent for hearing a song once, or at most twice, and recalling all the lyrics.

The explosion of outward artistic expression pushed me

deeper into the recesses of my world, where I felt ever more alienated and alone. I learned to play classical Spanish guitar on a nylon-stringed Gibson, which was no easy feat at nine years old. My teacher was my best friend and I adored him. Blind and hugely empathetic, Jorge was unlike anyone I had ever met. I found his Portuguese accent intriguing. The way he guided my hands on the chords was stellar. Normally I lost patience if I didn't get something right the first time around. If, after a few tries, I still didn't understand how to do something, I'd become despondent.

Jorge calmed me and taught me how to appreciate the process of learning. His mannerisms were a safe zone. For one hour every week, I felt secure and, dare I believe, loved. I had no defense. He was my refuge. I often sang Lovin' Spoonful's "You Didn't Have to Be So Nice" to myself when thinking of Jorge.

One of my favorite crafts was taking newspaper and magazine clippings of Twiggy and my favorite Motown bands and applying them to my lunchbox with shellac. Of course, the asinine kids at school made fun of me. My mother was no slave to fashion or art; she was, if anything, iconoclastic.

The one area that Mom didn't criticize or force me to be perfect in was my creative pursuits. As she allowed herself some slack in this area, I earned the same. She was the epitome of the Stone Poneys' song "Different Drum." Egging me on when I felt embarrassed, there was no mercy. I had to show up.

My peers didn't accept individual self-expression—and that added insult to injury. While I was insecure due to a lack of self-confidence, I discovered courage in my artistic abilities

Chapter 3 - A Recipe for Rage

and so refused to give in to group grope. The conflict for me was internal. I was stubborn enough to not give in to the demands of how I should act, dress, or express myself artistically; yet emotionally, I felt weighted down by a ball and chain.

The aggression issues that first surfaced when I was four persisted. They seemed to pop out left and right, from hidden corners at random times. I couldn't control myself no matter how hard I tried to suffocate my impulses. In fourth grade, I was strong, gangly, and tall, having already reached my adult height of five feet four inches.

I beat up a boy named Tommy Nolin on the concrete schoolyard. He was bullying me, calling me horrible racist names, so I threw my books at him, then stomped on his face, flinging rubber bands from my braces while the kids chanted, "Tommy got beat up by a girl."

When the neighborhood bully, a burly kid named Randy who weighed a ton and acted like a gorilla, pounced on my brother in the playground across from our apartment, I heard Richard desperately screaming my name. Our apartment faced the playground across the street, and our terrace door was usually open from spring to autumn when it wasn't raining out. I ran down the three stories as fast as I could, then dashed across the street to the monkey bars. I swung in a gymnast's round-off and slammed into Randy, knocking him down.

"Run, Richard, run, get home," I ordered, then dared the ape to fight me. He didn't; he slothed his way home.

I was like an undisciplined Peter Pan. I led the lost boys—the ragtag troupe of boys in the neighborhood, as I didn't relate to the girls, except for two of them who weren't friendly with each other—into adventures both dangerous and cretin.

Most of the girls were catty and mundane, yet I still sought to be liked by them. Everyone had known each other from the first grade through the sixth because no one ever moved away, or so it felt. I enjoyed our international group of classmates, who hailed from Israel, Germany, Holland, and India, to name a few countries. We had a beautiful rainbow of students from Black to Indian to Middle Eastern. I loved the diversity because, in my imagination, I traveled the world far and wide. Marco Polo was my hero. I dreamed of the day when I, too, would go over the sea to a faraway land.

I couldn't reconcile the silly concerns of the girls at school, and the way they gossiped very mean things behind one another's backs, with my values of being honest, of speaking from my heart, and of showing my sensitive nature. They spoke of boyfriends, how to snare a boy, or how to get one of them to kiss them. I couldn't care less. In that department I must have been deficient, because my timidity was palpable. Their favorite TV show was *I Dream of Jeannie,* while mine was *Outer Limits.* They liked frilly girlie-girl stuff; and me: science fiction, music, foreign travel, and the future. They talked of getting married and having babies; and me: time travel.

I had one friend who was a compassionate soul. A first-generation German who lived down the block, Roger was a good friend. He would come over to play, and we would actually talk about stuff and play board games together. No bullshit, no drama.

My family's building sat in front of the Long Island Railroad

Chapter 3 - A Recipe for Rage

train tracks. There was a sloping downhill slab of concrete that ran parallel to the kitchen windows in our building. One day after school, the boys and I found an empty shopping cart from Waldbaum's. I dared them to sit in the cart and travel at unknown speeds down the concrete hill. No one was fool enough to do so except me.

Down I spiraled at magnificent speed in a precarious metal supermarket cart whose wheels turned out the moment they hit rocky bits in the concrete. Before I could jump out (if that were even possible), the cart tipped and I was jettisoned onto the ground, hitting the metal fence that separated our building's property from the Long Island Railroad tracks. All at once, the six kitchen windows flew open with mothers sticking their heads out, clamoring to know what was wrong. People in China could probably hear my howls and wails. I have plenty of o' scars to prove my daredevil act failed.

The boys ran down to see if I was still alive, and soon enough my mother and a few others were downstairs to admonish the boys for allowing me to perform such an idiotic stunt (as if it had been their idea, not mine!). The mothers lifted me by my arms and legs and the boys followed to open the outside door that led to the elevator in the basement. My bruises were superficial and the black-and-blue marks took weeks to heal, but no bones were broken. Mom applied salve and gauze and propped me up in bed. No sooner had she kindly served me my favorite pistachio ice cream when she went into a rant about how I could do something like that to almost die.

I didn't know the difference between a prank and antisocial

behavior. One time, a friend and I ordered a pizza for the obnoxious neighbor who lived next door. We wanted to get back at her, a screaming Mimi. This woman, who worked the night shift as a nurse, never stopped yelling at her children from the moment she came home from work at two in the afternoon until they went to sleep. It was torturous. We could hear the pizza delivery man ring her bell. She screeched that she hadn't ordered the pie but had to pay anyway since there he was.

At other times the boys and I threw stones at alley cats or dropped raw eggs from our terrace onto unsuspecting passersby. We drowned an innocent turtle in liquid detergent, all in the name of science. The worst act I ever committed, though, was pinching a baby until he cried. The child was in his carriage outside the drugstore on Lefferts Boulevard while his mother shopped. I never told anyone of this particular crime.

Mom reserved Friday night dinner for both sets of grandparents, although more often than not Grandma Faye and Grandpa Irving came alone. Suddenly the pattern changed: Monday, Wednesday, and Friday, Grandma Faye was babysitting at our apartment. On weekends, Grandma Lily would watch us. What the heck was happening? I begged my mother to tell us. She refused as she slammed the door. I hardly saw my father.

I was confused. I knew something disastrous was happening in and to our family. The remnant of intuition still alive and breathing inside my inner core was terrified. Add to this the unsettling fact of Kitty Genovese's murder in Kew Gardens, two years earlier; mothers were on high alert. A lady on our floor survived an attack in her apartment at gunpoint. I shook every time I

Chapter 3 - A Recipe for Rage

passed her door on the way to the elevator. Stuff beyond my control or comprehension was going down fast. Andrea, our babysitter who was in her teens and seemed a tower of wisdom to my sensibilities, hugged me and let me weep in her arms. When I found out that her older brother Alex was being drafted to the horrific and incomprehensible Vietnam War (my mother was an avid anti-war protester, though not on the streets of D.C.—more like a protest couch potato who voiced her anti-war sentiments loud enough for me to comprehend and agree with), I wept for days worrying he'd come back in a casket.

With the external threats pounding in my head and the internal hemorrhaging of fear, I began having nightmares. I told Grandma about it. Her immense loving arms cradled me. She stroked my face and kissed me, but it didn't cure the torment I felt.

It was a recurring nightmare: large fire trucks arrived at our building right beneath our bedroom window to put out a massive fire spreading in our apartment. When I woke up sweating and freaking out, the firefighters were almost to my window, motioning me to hurry up and open it. I tried but couldn't. I fainted in the smoke and couldn't rescue my brother.

Chapter 4 – Lies, Alienation, and Creativity

Dix Hills, New York 1970–1972

We vacated our apartment at the end of elementary school (sixth grade for me, fourth grade for my brother). It was the end of one era in our lives. We headed to upstate New York for the summer holidays. I wasn't allowed to take my purple glitter butterfly-handlebar bike to our summer cabin, though.

Before leaving, Richard and I were granted permission to semi-vandalize our bedroom closet doors with gusto. We painted peace signs and affixed flower power stickers anywhere there was blank space. That was Mom's way of assuaging our anxiety and disapproval over our upcoming move to Nowhereland, Long Island.

Although by far *not* the most popular girl in my class, I did have those two close girlfriends Karen and Nancy whom I would miss terribly. Karen's mother knew me to be emotionally very pliable. Maybe even a pushover? I shared my anguish with them over this move and prayed they'd visit. They promised they would.

Long Island—that is, Dix Hills—was a one-hour train or car ride away. The Long Island Expressway ended ten exits past Dix Hills, and then that was it, a dead end. We were located way too far for my friends' parents to drop their kids off for a weekend.

My parents said they wanted to include my brother and me in the decision-making process as to where we'd move. A year earlier, when house hunting began in earnest, we actually did inspect a few homes as a family. I was drawn to a beautiful 1940s vintage two-story stone house with a pitched roof in Englewood, New Jersey. It was nestled in the woods and surrounded by high elms, weeping willows, and oak trees, located far away from road noise and shopping malls. That was my first choice.

Then, nothing. Without showing us where the last house was located, our parents made a decision. The family moved into a sterile, newly built development, a cookie-cutter suburban neighborhood with planted trees where the original majestics had been torn out. We lived in a cul-de-sac, literally devoid of life. Right next to our home was a mound, which we were told was a former Native American burial ground.

Shut out from city life and burdened with making the best of a dire situation, I sat on the curb most of the summer. My solace was listening to Led Zeppelin, Jethro Tull, the Who, and Rod Stewart on my transistor. I was starved for civilization and depressed. There was only so much radio and so many *Circus* magazines I could read on the sweltering curb.

By this point in my life, I had been scribbling in a diary. It was under lock and key in case my meddlesome brother decided to ransack my things. He jeopardized my boundaries surreptitiously. Why would he be any different from Mom, who had practically none at all? The rationale for my possessiveness over "things" was that they were tangible. I could hold on to them in place of parental love that was ephemeral at best and twisted at worst. I could claim them as I genuinely wished to be claimed.

Chapter 4 - Lies, Alienation, and Creativity

Richard needed continual reprimanding. I tried convincing him that what he was or wasn't doing was right or wrong or morally repugnant. He was stubborn, like Mom. I was talking to the wall.

I sensed it was a double standard for me! I didn't know how to reconcile my high-and-mighty ethical and moralistic side with the vengeful, and morose side. I was so afraid of that part of me that I didn't dare write about it in my diary for fear of being called a fraud. People generally thought of me as a strong-willed, outspoken individualist whose head was in the clouds. I was distraught at the mere notion of having a split personality.

Unable to take a break from the heaviness—the loneliness and boredom, the humidity and oppressive ninety-five-degree days—I distracted myself with painting. The black-and-white Peter Max wallpaper motif Mom had put up in my room was primed for coloring in.

I knew no one except for one girl my age who lived down the road, but she wasn't my type of friend. We had nothing in common except that she hailed from the city. She hadn't ever heard of FM radio, ugh! What was a city kid like me supposed to do in a development where the sparse teenage population had never heard of Laura Nyro's deep, soulful crooning or "Sunshine of Your Love" by Cream —Britain's supergroup with Eric Clapton, Jack Bruce, and Ginger Baker? None of my neighborhood adult peers had ever been to New York City. Ever! That was a spooky place for those hicks. Middle school was still four weeks away. I thought of Lord Alfred Tennyson's "I must lose myself in action, lest I wither in despair."

Richard seemed to be in his own daydreamy world and didn't seem to mind the move. Since he had attended a neighborhood day camp, he had friends before the school year began—fifth-grade elementary. He was set.

I survived seventh grade at the FDR-ranch-style middle school that looked like an extended version of one of the many suburban houses in that part of the township of Huntington. The year went along relatively smoothly. A few things struck me, though, in the wrong way.

During the first semester, girls weren't allowed to wear jeans or pants to school! What the heck? I felt as if I had been extradited to a deprived country. During the second half of the year we were liberated; I wore tie-dyed jeans that made the principal's eyes pop like googly eyes. Many of the kids, I noted, were blond-haired with blue eyes and wore crosses. I was smothered by German Barbie and Ken lookalikes. I noticed there were hardly any brown people or Asians, unlike my school in Queens. I didn't have words for this; I just intuitively knew I didn't belong there and it was wrong!

I had excellent grades, over 95 in all subjects, and excelled in English and Spanish. I hadn't made acquaintances so much as sifted through people until I found a couple of good friends: Claudia and Roger. For a few months I even had a short fling, if one could call it that, with Paul, whose locker was next to mine. He gave me a gold-plated heart necklace that said "Elise + Paul forever." We held hands in public but didn't dare kiss; that was done in secret. He was the very first boy that I could call a "boyfriend," someone I had a crush on, someone who reciprocated my feelings.

Chapter 4 - Lies, Alienation, and Creativity

Valentine's Day 1971

From the yellow Princess rotary dial phone located on a countertop in our kitchen, Mom rang me at my friend's house, where I was hanging out for the day.

"You need to come home early," she upbraided me in her gravelly Merit cigarette voice. Coughing loudly in my ear, she said, "There's something Dad and I want to tell you." There was a finality in her voice, a tone she used when she was going to a) punish me, or b) download some hey-you-won't-like-this kind of news. Somewhere deep inside I knew the worst was yet to come, but I couldn't define what kind of worse! All the rings and tones of her ever-changing moods were familiar to me, yet this finality made me retreat into the safest zone I knew—a hidden cubicle nestled between my belly and my heart. A place where, when I closed my eyes, I could see specks of dust mites turn into white flashing lights while little me swirled into a soft ice cream cone.

"No, I'm hanging out with Debby. Her mom is making dinner for us. I'll come home at 8:00 like we said."

"No, you won't," she reproached me. "You will come home right now." Mom's voice got higher by a few octaves.

"Why? Give me one good reason why," I provoked her. I wasn't going to give in that easily. Who did she think she was, bossing me around as if I were a little kid? She handed the phone to my father, which was strange. In a softer tone, he pleaded for me to listen to my mother. Debby's older sister drove me home. I was reluctant to find out what was wrong, because something definitely was not right!

The lovey-dovey Valentine's Day cards my parents wrote

to each other sat atop the fireplace mantel. Ever since I was in the fifth grade, it felt as if my parents lived separate lives, except for the group outings on weekends or if our grandparents were over. They hardly spent weekday evenings together. Richard and I went by bus from school to home, did our homework (well, I did my homework while he rattled off excuses why he couldn't), then I set the table and helped Mom prepare dinner. Family dinners ceased when we moved to Long Island.

For them to sit us both down at the same time had to be something monumental. They solemnly sat across from Richard and me. Richard and I squirmed and glanced at each other with foreboding. We were ordered to remain on the couch. Something ominous was about to go down.

Then *WHAMMO!*

Mom looked nervously at Dad, whose face hung in shame. No more smiles or jokes, just guilty silence. She took the lead. "Your father and I have something to tell you both." Richard and I became anxious. I reflexively grabbed his hand.

"We are getting a divorce." Dad still said nothing. He could hardly lift his head to look at us.

Stuttering, I managed to ask in a whisper, "When are you leaving, Dad?" since dads were the ones who left in these situations.

He dropped the bombshell. "Tonight."

I wanted to keep company with absolutely no one on the face of the Earth. I let go of Richard's hand and immediately went into an uncontrollable frenzy, screaming, "You're both a bunch of fucking liars. How could you give each other Valentine's Day

Chapter 4 - Lies, Alienation, and Creativity

cards and then lie to our faces? You're fucking insane and sick in the head. Both of you. I hate you both."

My heart ached and pounded, my mind shattered like a kaleidoscope, thousands of family images blurred in my brain. Then, as if in a freefall drop from an airplane with too many air pockets, I collapsed inside. All trust vanished in an instant. All hope in the human race and its goodness fizzled out. It was my first conscious exposure to disconnection. Like a satellite orb cut off from the mothership, I was left to find my way back to Earth. My eleven-year-old brother just sat there with silent tears streaming down his cheeks.

Until that moment I had no clue what naked fear or the depths of my own terrifying screams sounded like, because I hadn't screamed like that ever before.

Stunned at my volatility, my parents sat immobilized.

I managed one last swipe: "You used Richard and me like pawns in your messed-up game of playing family."

My throat parched and spent, I grabbed my brother's hand and squeezed so hard that blood vessels seemed to pop from his forehead. In grief, I shouted and kicked the living room table, and we both fell into a crying fit. I wished I could protect my brother and me from this fate, which was worse than anything else we had known up to that point in our tender lives. I knew instinctively that we would have to fend for ourselves. As Dad walked out the door for the last time in his life, I ran screaming down the hallway after him. My brother wouldn't let him go, like a dog whose master tries shaking the animal off and finally abandons it. As the door thumped in its jamb, the music stopped dead on the turntable of my inner ear. No more Benny Goodman, Gene Krupa, Al Jolson. No more Daddy whistling, snapping his fingers, tapping his feet, and shaking his index finger like a metronome to his music.

No more bellowing, "Shut off that music already!" No more jokes when all I wanted was for him to take me seriously.

The miserable constellation of betrayal and deceit resulted in my choking and hyperventilating. I couldn't breathe. Mom called the ambulance and I was rushed to the hospital. On the stretcher, fighting for every breath of my life, I awoke to sounds of muffled voices, official voices. People in white uniforms were fussing over me. In a deep trancelike state, it dawned on me that I was flat out in the hospital. Mom scoured the linoleum with her cowboy boots. I didn't know where Richard was, but Mom was in and out of the room to smoke her Merits like a fiend in the hallway, while the apparatus sat like an octopus on a black metal rotating box, waiting to suffocate me with its plastic tentacles. This ugly contraption was going to give me the breath of life, O_2. Mom came back into the room with a cup of steaming burnt Nescafé in a plastic cup. She was all teary, racked with guilt. Then I saw Richard, frightened and weeping, pulling on Mom's culottes.

"What happened, Mom? How did I...?" I felt my chest caving in as I grasped for precious sips of air. I couldn't finish my sentence. It petrified me, and within seconds I needed the oxygen mask. The medication the nurse gave me filtered inside the atomizer and had a peppery, sour aftertaste that lingered long enough to open my lungs while suppressing my taste buds.

What I needed to get back was the routine act of inhalation

Chapter 4 - Lies, Alienation, and Creativity

and exhalation. Quickly! Apparently, I had hyperventilated to the point of not being able to draw in air. Everyone in my family dreaded the hospital except me. I wasn't so much anti-hospital as I was anti-blood, guts, gore, open wounds, and body parts. Hospitals in and of themselves were antiseptic places that didn't stir my emotions. They were neutral ground. I have never broken a bone nor had an operation besides the fun one when I was three. I had my tonsils removed as all kids seemed to have done at the start of the new decade, *the sixties*. What I remember of that time was eating loads of sherbet.

Because of my hyperventilation, the hospital was graced with my presence for over a week. I was put on a respirator. My father did not come to visit me. The connection between my parents was severed. I feared it was also gone with me and my brother. I longed for comfort from my Dad's arms, but he wasn't around. Paul, who was now my best bud (he'd discovered he was gay), and a troupe of friends visited me every night. They brought joints for us to smoke in the room. We did and weren't caught. Despite the smoking, I didn't have another asthma attack.

Claudia's parents were the only ones amongst my friends who had divorced. She was a lifesaver during the time immediately after I returned from the hospital.

Claudia invited me for a sleepover so that her mother, who was an excellent communicator with an earthy approach, could help me during this catastrophic time. She sat me down at the kitchen table after I unpacked.

"Elise, look your mother went through something awful, as far as I could tell and now so are you", claimed Claudia's black-haired statuesque mom. Her eyes pierced mine. "When I got divorced from Claudia's father I had to raise the girls on my own and wasn't even there all the time as I had to work. Since you're the eldest, you're going to have to look out for your brother and yourself now." She paused as tears swelled in my eyes.

"But I already do that. I've been doing that my whole life and I have no one. No one!" I blurted. I didn't want to take care of my brother. Who was going to take care of me?

Claudia chimed in, "You're going to go through a lot of phases until you can find a way to get back to normal." Then with a more sympathetic tone, "You have us Elise, you have us so you're not alone", she reassured me as she held my hand in both of hers.

Claudia's sister was a force of good as well. Five years older than us, she survived her parent's divorce unscathed. That's probably due to the mature approach they embraced, unlike my bipolar mother, who'd been ranting since I was born.

Mom had the wherewithal to take me to a therapist upon my release from the hospital. The doctors there recommended I be put on antidepressants for a year following the divorce. I also visited a clinical psychologist, whom I outwitted with lies. That kind of help was just an excuse for me to get out of the house and talk stream-of-consciousness. It wasn't by any means a cure to the wretchedness and brokenness I felt inside.

After a few months, once we sort of settled into the newness of living without Dad, Richard and I began to visit him every weekend. At first he would drive out to the island on a Friday after school and bring us back to the city to his bachelor pad, then return us on Sunday night. One day that arrangement came

Chapter 4 - Lies, Alienation, and Creativity

to a crashing halt. I never knew why. Against our will, Richard and I had to take the Long Island Railroad round-trip alone to visit Dad. I dreaded those trips and hated the dirty train. We'd be sullen and emotionally depleted on those rides. Nothing was sadder than seeing my baby brother's eyes filled with torment. We were in an abyss with no escape and I certainly was in no position to come to his rescue. I was no longer the older sister he could look up to.

I was still processing this enormous loss a few months later when Mom cavalierly dropped the news that Grandma Faye would be watching us for a month. Huh? Why? So she could gallivant in swinging London with her best friend, Lillian—one of the old crowd, also then divorced, and mother to Stephonic.

My grades went to hell after the divorce. I lost interest in Spanish and barely passed my classes. Marijuana and hashish became my companions. I was obstreperous, and on more than one occasion, I hopped out of my bedroom window and hitched a ride to friends' houses. Once, I convinced an acquaintance to hitch with me to Florida, for the fun of picking up fresh oranges and then returning with a pack of them stuffed in our backpacks. Maria slept over at my house so we could make a smooth getaway.

I was ever the organizer and project planner, so I wrapped up five PB&J sandwiches in Saran Wrap and took a glass container—one that looked like a small Mason jar—and stuffed it with freshly rolled joints. We probably had twenty packed tightly in there for the road. My idea was to convey to drivers that we'd have a good time on the trip: we'd all smoke weed together. Maria and I wore scant T-shirts under our winter jackets and sweaters so we could peel them off as we drove south on I-95 toward the hot and muggy lands of swampy Florida. Our final destination was Miami, but we made it only to exit 32 near Little Neck Parkway in Queens. A cop car came whirring down the expressway, blaring a siren and blinding us with its blue and red disco light atop the hood. He pulled us over and admonished us for hitchhiking, asking if we didn't know how dangerous it was for two young girls to be out, especially in the middle of the night.

A few hours later, both sets of parents drove the thirty or so minutes to the police station in Nassau County to pick us up. We had to give up my joints, which I was really angry about. I offered the cops our peanut butter and jelly sandwiches because I knew from the TV series *Serpico* that they liked coffee and doughnuts, and I figured the sandwiches would hit their sweet tooth. But nah, they passed on it, and we waved goodbye.

On the way back home without preamble, Mom blurted out, "Lillian and I are definitely going to London so Grandma is going to watch you for two weeks."

"What the heck Mom? We didn't even have enough money for heat last winter and now you're going to Europe!" I exclaimed in utter bewilderment.

"Well Lillian is paying for a big chunk of the trip so don't you worry your sweet little head about it, okay", she stated not as a question rather as a final 'stop asking any more questions'.

"Well fine then but tell Grandma that I will not take care of Richard's stuff."

Grandma Faye made the wrong decision in agreeing with Mom to watch me and Richard. It was on one of my getaway

Chapter 4 - Lies, Alienation, and Creativity

escapades that my grandmother almost had a heart attack when she discovered I was not asleep in my bedroom as I should have been. It scared her enough that when I arrived home much later, all ragged and stoned from partying into the morning, and mumbled a "Hi, Grandma," she flew into a fitful screaming match with herself while brandishing the utterly useless threat of grounding me.

From the kitchen, which had a cutout that led to the living room, Grandma bellowed at the top of her lungs, "You will not ever run away and have one of those orgies, Elise, or I'll smack you harder than your mother ever did and you won't know what hit you." I peered through the alcove from the hallway to see her completely red face.

I couldn't help but crack up, which is the worst thing one can do when someone is having a meltdown. Grandma pronounced the word *orgy* as *or-ghee*. She ran after me with impressive speed (given that she was a bit overweight and rather small at five foot, like many immigrant grandparents of the day). She slapped my face! Hard. That was the first and last time in her entire life she raised a hand to me.

Grandma was unable to discipline me and was relieved to get back home and the hell away from us. Mom returned from the U.K. with Mary Quant makeup and Twiggy-style miniskirts for me. She had tins of Fortnum & Mason teas and mint jelly for the lamb shanks she would never cook. As if these gifts were going to help me! She drooled over all the groovy men she met in London's Soho district and at the famed jazz club Ronnie Scott's. I wanted to hear more about London, its people, the sights.

"Did you go to Abbey Road?" I wanted to know. No, she hadn't.

After that she began dating nonstop. Everyone I really liked as a potential new dad, she dumped. She articulated in crude terms why she left the men I admired, her reasoning boiling down to sex, and she indiscriminately shared her antics with me. As a teen going through puberty, I was fortunate to have a mother without hangups on the topic of sexuality. She taught me about menstruation before it happened so I was prepared. Once I became "a woman," she explained the dangers of teenage pregnancy and offered to buy me the Pill. But the burdensome weight of her confiding in me about her private life as if I were her best girlfriend left scars for decades.

One day after school, I shakily put the key in the lock. I could hear Mom's ear-piercing ululations. *What now?* I cringed as my heart palpitated. I tried making myself invisible by tiptoeing down the hallway. I could tell an overshare was coming.

"Get over here and listen to this, Elise," she roared. I timidly stood in the archway between the dining room and kitchen. She jumped up and jammed the phone into my face, screaming to the person on the other end, "Go on, tell her what you told me." Then she threw the phone off its cradle and broke the receiver.

In a torrent of *fucks*, *bastards*, *scumbags*, and other delightful vulgarities, she bellowed that the woman who called had Dad's baby. He had been living a double life while Mom and Dad were still married. I stood frozen in the alcove. Eventually she quieted down and composed herself. As if on cue, I leaned in to comfort her, hold her, and shake the shakes out of her.

From that moment on, unconsciously, I put my father on trial. He could not catch a break from me as I sentenced him to a life of regret and guilt.

Chapter 4 - Lies, Alienation, and Creativity

Three months later, my beloved grandmother died. Grandma Faye and I had an unspoken bond of love. We didn't talk about my problems with my parents or friends. She wasn't conversant in that or perhaps was unprepared to console me verbally. Instead, she showed unconditional love through caresses and cooking. Although our last encounter almost threw her over the edge, her reaction didn't take away from the fact that I loved her deeply.

Though still living in my mother's home, at fourteen I became my own boss. Mom had relinquished any jurisdiction over me.

Two months after Grandma died, I felt as if an angel saved me. I fell in "puppy love" at a concert at the Nassau Coliseum when I spotted Joshua and his three friends. They were flirting with Claudia and me. I could've chosen any one of them—Steve, the lanky brown-haired one who sort of looked like Neil Young; or Ray, a good-looking strawberry blonde with dark brown eyes and the cutest freckles. He was feisty, but Joshua won me over with his confidence and sex appeal. His thick, black, wavy hair fell over the side of his square face. He had dimples when he smiled, and his almond-shaped, hazel-colored eyes pierced me. He reminded me of Steve Winwood of Traffic. His full lips were sweet, as was his shy smile. These boys were a year older than us.

Josh and I were like best friends with a little extra since we made out. I could pour my heart and soul out to him without fear of double-dealing. He was innocent and brave-hearted; a kind-of protector in a way.

At first we visited each other every Saturday, and then it became Saturdays and Sundays. He lived in Bellmore, a good thirty minutes' drive west. Every other weekend he'd visit me and on alternate weekends I would go to his house. After a few months, his parents allowed us to spend the night at each other's homes; when I told my mother I didn't need her permission for anything, she backed off. Josh and I set up a date for the following weekend when his older brother would drive me home.

One of the reasons my mother agreed to give me free reign was that I called her bluff. She was screaming at something or other, and I had had enough of being taunted. Out of control, she raged and began throwing the contents of her bag while running to my bedroom: a toiletry bag, keys, a wallet, a brush, random plastic utensils, tissue. On a rampage to destroy, she burst into my bedroom.

Grabbing her by her thin wrists, I pinned her to the wall: "If you ever dare raise a hand toward me again, I will literally kill you," I said evenly. A cold darkness grew over me. I had just crossed a line and there was no return. "I've put up with your abuse for fourteen years, and today it's over. Do you read me? Over and out," I said, squinting at her pupils as they dilated.

I dove into writing poetry and recording my dreams while continuing to journal. I rediscovered painting, sculpting, and crocheting. The relationship with Joshua lasted one year but probably would've gone on many more years had it not been for my mother fucking everything up.

Out of the blue, Mom announced her engagement to Joshua's older brother Mike, who was only twenty-three! Mom was thirty-five and wild to the core. I cannot, could not stomach the idea of staying in love with my stepuncle! That's what Joshua would become in relation to me after his brother married my mother.

I was in shock, and I felt betrayed. How could my mother do this? It was madness that I had to break up with the boy I loved.

Chapter 4 - Lies, Alienation, and Creativity

The pressure was on before the wedding. Joshua's mom became bitchy toward me. Whenever she could, she'd make nasty comments to tear at my vulnerabilities, like "Your mother is a used car and my son should have nothing to do with her" or "Over my dead body will I allow my son to marry your mother." She continued to viciously attack her, which prevented me from showing her the love and compassion I previously demonstrated. Little did I know that she was yet another narcissist in the line of narcissists I grew up with. My relationship with her deteriorated. She viciously attacked my mother, which prevented me from showing her the love and compassion I previously held for her.

I had to break up with Joshua, as I could find no moral reason to continue. The strained relationship with his brother, whom I liked but didn't want as a stepfather; the ever-increasing vitriol of his mother; and the weirdness of being an inherited relative to the boy I loved was too much to bear. My father encouraged the breakup also. Not that he was in any position to give moral advice or support, but he did anyway. This scenario was just too much, even for the master con man.

Chapter 5 - My Sexual Revolution

The Basement 1972–1973

Sex, drugs, and rock 'n' roll were the anthem of the seventies and formed much of my teenage experience. It made up the tapestry that would shape and propel me to become a creative experimentalist in the bedroom, a staunch adventurer in life, and a risk-taker in my career.

My parents spoke liberally about sex. They used loose phraseology and peppered conversations and jokes with sexual innuendos. Although it was their freewheeling embrace of the times—as if their sexuality had been bottled up until the 1970s, when society permitted them to go apeshit—I found it unnerving.

I grew up as a tomboy without the American dogma of what a girl should dress like, behave like, or be. I was on an all-boys' baseball team in elementary school. My Dad did dishes, the laundry, and the cleaning in our home. Mom took me with her on weekends to wholesale interior design showrooms in the 57 Building in Manhattan. I was exposed to homosexuality from a very early age and liked the men who were effeminate. One of Mom's friends was bisexual. I remember hearing that lady talk about kissing another woman. I didn't blink an eye, nor was I shocked. I related to the uncommon. I wanted to be androgynous. David Bowie naturally became my idol.

How relieved I was to finally find my tribe of friends at the beginning of eighth grade—artsy, socially responsible (yet emotionally dysfunctional) misfits. We considered any sort of sexual experiment a rite of passage. Given the fact that this was the age of Women's Lib and AIDS was nowhere yet on the horizon, we took full advantage of the times and lived it up as if there were no tomorrow!

Gays with lesbians, bisexuals with gays of either gender, same-sex with a heterosexual, hetero couples with a bisexual, transvestites with straights—you name it, we tried it. We did it anywhere: bathrooms in our friends' parents' homes, on the school football field, in the school washrooms, on the highways, in the buses, in the mall in some sleazy little corner. Anywhere was okay as long as someone could potentially see what we were doing. Mostly though, we played in my basement.

Exhibitionism was the rage. Whether we were Glitter freaks listening to David Bowie or innocent Incredible String Band hippie types, we all screwed our way through junior high school. Some girls had "done it" at fourteen, even thirteen. We had choices: Screw your way out of boredom, do soft drugs, or listen to rock 'n' roll; enough of it to fill ten of those dorky football fields where none of my friends ventured.

Because of my crowd of friends, I established footing in my environment. I had a place—if not geographically, then certainly within this group of my choosing.

Most of them were at least a year older, in ninth or tenth grade. We'd meet in my unfinished basement, which reeked of detergent, damp concrete, and leftover winter chill. We all got

Chapter 5 - My Sexual Revolution

together on the weekends and painted the entire underground space. Rugs were donated; we hung black lights and black light posters to honor the rock bands we worshipped, like Pink Floyd, Yes, Led Zeppelin, the Who, Ziggy Stardust and the Spiders from Mars, Marc Bolan, Genesis. We named our spot "The Den of Iniquity." It was our secret meeting place for smoking pot, doing bongs, and experimenting with one another sexually.

The crew included Ian, a striking, red-haired, freckle-face activist and social worker who stood up for migrant workers' rights. He was humorous and a bit of a loner. Six-foot-four lanky Mark had extraordinarily long fingers but didn't play any instrument. He was our resident poet and looked precisely like Joey Ramone. Mark was extremely shy, yet once he got going, was wry and acutely critical of society. I was super hot for Logan, who looked like a British rocker with pale white skin and a mop of curly, dirty-blond hair. He wore John Lennon eyeglasses and a gray Mao-inspired military cap (but wasn't a communist). His black leather motorcycle jacket hung lazily on his thin yet muscular frame. Deeply intellectual and cerebral, he offered up the best conversations when we got stoned.

Kathy was the shortest in our gang, even shorter than me, and I was five feet four inches. Her outstanding feature was her XXL boobs that shot out like bazookas. She wore a crooked part in her hair, and her unusual nose was a source of fascination, with nostrils in a constant state of flare. "Does life continuously perturb her?" I wondered. Her heart-shaped mouth curled at the edges when she laughed. Kathy was an experimental macramé artist enamored with Bob Dylan and Joni Mitchell.

Betty and Diane were a lesbian couple who kept to themselves but joined us when inspired to be around others. Betty, who was a jokester, and Diane, her opposite—earnest and studious—reminded us of Cheech and Chong. Betty was six feet tall and skinny like Patti Smith, with straggly black hair and longish bangs that covered her brown eyes. She wore what seemed to be her uniform: jeans, black tee, and black satin baseball jacket. Diane had thick cropped blonde hair worn all combed back as if in a ponytail. Her inquisitive green eyes and honey-colored skin attracted men until she repelled them, so she resorted to wearing sunglasses, even indoors. In that way, she didn't have to look at the boys who flirted with her.

Diane once took me to the side in the football field in back of our HS and admitted, "Elise your bright sunshiny nature blinds me. It's as if I need to be positive around you and I can't do that."

I was deeply hurt by the words that stung but more than the words by her matter-of-fact acceptance of her own melancholia. I too had bouts of depression but internally I was ever the optimist, the fool in the Tarot.

There was one standout in the bunch, and that was Michelle. When we met, we immediately bonded; she became my best friend of the entire group. I admired her élan and class and latched onto her genius mind. As a Francophile, she listened to musicians I hadn't heard of: Edith Piaf and Erik Satie. My musical diet consisted of 1940s jazz and a little Miles, Motown R&B, Brit pop and rock, and some classical. Hearing chanson and modern classical was like living in an alternative reality. Both artists influenced me profoundly by igniting the childhood yearning to travel to far-off places. My heart leaped at the cadence of Piaf's defiant voice as she sang "*Non, Je Ne Regrette Rien.*" I related to her grit and insistence that no one should pity her miserable childhood of abandonment and poverty.

Satie's "Gymnopedies" transported me to a world of pensive reclusiveness. Floating to his tranquil piano composition, I imagined myself in the Montmartre section of Paris at a literary salon amongst writers. Around this time, I realized I wanted to write when I grew up.

My introduction to French literature was again thanks to Miche (my French nickname for her). Miche was statuesque and mature-looking—at least seventeen in my book. Blonde wavy hair framed her oval face and deep-set blue eyes. She applied a fake beauty mark on her left cheek with an eyebrow pencil and smoked Kools from an ivory cigarette holder, straight out of the 1940s. She was a beatnik twenty years after the fact. She wore only black. That was pretty far-out.

With Miche, I needed a dictionary. Her near Oxford-level vocabulary inspired me to master and absorb the meanings of words I had never spoken. To learn from a close friend was, to me, the epitome and meaning of friendship. God knows I was starved of intellectual stimulation in my home. I was mesmerized by her. For the life of me, I couldn't figure out how she had access to arcane knowledge. Her parents were typical suburbanites, so they weren't the ones who could take credit, and she was their lone child.

Miche encouraged me to read the French philosophers, from Sartre to Voltaire, well before we were obliged to do so in school. We argued over one thing only, and that was literature. I was adamant about Russian literature, which I fancied far more than the French with one exception: Colette. Having discovered her book *Cheri* at about the same time as I discovered my own sexuality, I wasn't opposed to the idea of experimenting with the same gender. Russian authors were deeply emotive, enmeshed in their surroundings and the lives of others in ways more earthy, more melancholic than the French.

I had read about Timothy Leary's experiments with the mind-altering substance LSD. He was a brilliant Harvard psychologist whose words got wedged in my impressionable mind. "You're only as young as the last time you changed your mind" and "Women who seek to be equal with men lack ambition." I knew I had to try LSD.

And so, one ordinary weekend evening, I invited Kathy to sleep over so we could drop some LSD, because Miche wouldn't do it. I was a risk-taker on many levels yet maintained common sense, so I read in advance about some of the effects of the drug, such as hallucinations and mind-altering time and depth perception. That seemed cool.

We dropped the LSD and sat cross-legged on my yellow shag carpet in my bedroom, our knees touching. The room itself was psychedelic without taking anything because of the Peter Max wallpaper which was now fully colored in. I instructed Kathy to breathe deeply, following my direction. I had recently read Ram Dass's best-selling book, *Be Here Now,* so I knew about meditation, breathing, and other Indian exercises for the body, mind, and soul. Not that I knew how to meditate the right way. I felt my

Chapter 5 - My Sexual Revolution

breath was too quick, and I didn't know quite how to move the air from the lower part of my abdomen to the upper part of my lungs.

The drug must have kicked in, because the next thing I remembered was Kathy unbuttoning her blouse. I wasn't attracted to her, nor did I tell her to do so. She insisted she was hot. I was seeing all kinds of colors and shapes and couldn't focus on her enough to button her shirt for her. Even if I did, she would unbutton it immediately. It was like being on a merry-go-round.

At some point, I was getting bored with her performance, so I went to the bathroom. My brother was sound asleep in his room, as were my mother and stepfather in the master bedroom. Looking in the mirror was a trip in itself. Every pore on my face produced a teardrop. Tears were pouring out as my dilated eyes became teal, then purple, then indigo, then navy blue. The bathtub had no shower curtain or glass door to it. It was bare, as were the walls. Yet I saw flowers and a lush jungle being born on the walls.

I have no idea how long I was there. Suddenly I heard a shrill scream from my mother's room.

I unlocked the bathroom door and tiptoed (or so I thought) to my room first, to see where Kathy was; logic was at work here. Not there! I ventured into my mother's bedroom, and there she was, jumping on my parents' bed. Nude!

My stepfather's eyes almost fell out of their sockets, like those of a bobblehead dashboard doll. My brother got into the fray as well. I guess it was the first time he saw a girl naked. I mean, who could resist? As soon as he got a good glimpse of her,

Mom sent Richard right back to his room. And a good overview he did get, as the lights were now on at both night tables.

Alarmed that I had to play straight to convince my mother that I wasn't stoned, I feigned innocence, as if I had no idea what was going on. "Mom, Kathy and I smoked a joint. She's just stoned. I guess she never did it before", I shrugged it off. Mom was pissed off, but not in a way where she'd throw a tantrum or fly off the handle. She was, after all, a bleeding-heart hippie liberal and was aware that my friends and I smoked pot. What angered her was being woken up by a naked girl.

I offered to help get Kathy down from the bed, where her tits were flying in all directions. I was in hysterics and couldn't stop myself, though. The sight of her left Mom speechless, probably one of the few times in her entire life!

We dragged Kathy to my bedroom and tried to put her clothes on—no such luck. The moment one of us got some garment zipped or buttoned up, Kathy would tear it off. I have no clue how long this went on, but it was no fun for me. After several attempts, Mom gave up and decided to call Kathy's mother. I pleaded with her not to, as her mom was not going to be sympathetic.

She got the phone number out of me and dialed. Kathy's LSD trip was about one thing only: taking off her clothes, freeing herself from any garments. Maybe she was an Earth goddess trying to return to the land. She did macramé, after all.

Her mother arrived sometime near 3:00 a.m. I only know the time because my stepfather was yelling it out and telling us all to be quiet, he wanted to go back to sleep.

Chapter 5 - My Sexual Revolution

As Kathy's mother walked to my room, I tried alerting her to what was to follow: her daughter insisting on taking off her clothes. I felt like a little shit, but I had to save my ass. I never mentioned it was LSD. To soften the blow, I just said we smoked some pot. That was the truth! Her mom wasn't savvy enough to know that pot wouldn't have any such effect. Her mom became adamantly curious, demanding to know why I wasn't reacting the same way. Why were my clothes still on?

Shrugging my shoulders while pinning Kathy to the wall, I helped her mom dress her. Then the three of us dragged her outside and put her into her mother's Chevy.

Mom went back to sleep, but my brother was curious and wanted to know every detail. I told him I couldn't talk; I was wasted and would tell him in the morning. I spent the rest of the trip painting, actually squirting my yellow carpet with acrylics—orange and red.

My Father's Place, Roslyn, New York 1973
I took after my father in the music department. While he was still living with us, he snuck me into many concerts. He was the East Coast sales rep for Panasonic and received swag in the form of concert tickets. Before I was twelve, I saw Herman's Hermits, Three Dog Night, and Iron Butterfly live. I, too, collected records.

When we still lived in the city, Dad would take me on Saturdays to the main drag in Forest Hills, one town away from Kew Gardens. With my allowance money, I'd buy 45s. I had five boxes filled with 45s—hit songs from the Monkees, the Beatles, the Supremes, Petula Clark, Nancy Sinatra, and a full collection of Motown from the Temptations, Four Tops, Marvin Gaye, Mary Wells, and so many others. By the time we moved to Long Island, I had the beginnings of a small album collection. By 1973, I had over a thousand LPs alphabetically arranged. They took up the space from the window to the door, practically filling up the entire wall.

Besides the great stadiums such as Nassau Coliseum and Madison Square Garden, there were three clubs I usually hitchhiked to: Kenny's Castaways and Max's Kansas City in Manhattan and My Father's Place on Long Island. My Father's Place was in Roslyn, one of the five towns on Long Island (and an unlikely locale for a venue). It opened in 1971 and featured some of the best bands.

The small, intimate club seated no more than 150 people at most, just like in a jazz club. I have no idea how I faked my ID, but come hell or high water, I was going to get in to hear Bruce Springsteen, whose debut album, *Greetings From Asbury Park*, was on my hit list.

All of my friends were in high school, and some already had driver's licenses. Pam was one of them. She had never been to a live concert and was game, so she agreed to drive to the club. On the way there, we spoke about our futures upon graduation. I learned she was going into the military. I told her I was going to be a rock 'n' roll journalist.

The sexual play my friends and I engaged in wasn't really like flirting. Sex just happened when we were together. It felt like Pam was attracted to me, and it was in a category by itself. She hinted that she liked girls. That was far-out.

We got into the club and sat about one hundred feet away from The Boss. The seating was so close that I felt squashed. To my left was a beautiful Black man, and to my right, Pam, whose hand was casually running up and down my arm. I allowed her to touch me. The lights went dim; we ordered some beers, anticipating a great show. Bruce and the E Street Band started with "Blinded by the Light." When Clarence Clemons played saxophone on "Spirit in the Night," I lost it. Groovin' to the music, Pam, me, and the man seemed to meld as one.

When the set was over, we decided to go back to the man's place to have a ménage à trois. Once undressed, Pam and I naturally met each other's lips. We were kissing and petting. Our male friend stayed on my side since Pam had no interest in him. I would occasionally show him some attention—just enough so I could turn back toward Pam. I had a realization. This girl was so much gentler than most of the boys I had balled. She was kind in her touch and moved slowly. There was no urgency to screw. That felt so good, almost a relief. As if I didn't have to be on the defense.

Maybe I was bi or pan after all?

Chapter 6 – Fucking My Way Through Europe

Sweet Sixteen Tour, July–August 1973

Rachel, my wacky stepmom, is fourteen years older than me. She sometimes acted like my best girlfriend. Well, that was in front of my face. We often argued but not as much as I did with my Dad, who had turned into a resolute conservative. Compared with her, he was out of place and old-fashioned. I couldn't understand how he'd married a girl whose flagrantly wild spirit was almost identical to mine. Then again, it's not for teenagers to follow their parents; it's vice versa. And that was the trouble.

I studied my own family and the parents of my numerous friends and acquaintances under a microscope. Most adults didn't have a clue, some had no interest, and others were just darned scared out of their wits over their childrens' budding sexuality and coming of age. These prudes were in denial, nine feet deep, and warned my friends to stay away from me. Apparently, Kathy's mom spoke with some of the other moms at school during a PTA meeting and spread the word that "Elise is a bad influence." I think three or four of my so-called friends dropped out of sight. I couldn't have cared less, except for having to travel to the city alone.

My father was still addicted to 1930s pop-jazz, and everyone in his vicinity was tortured by those scratchy Al Jolson-y throwaway tunes that he played for years on end. And if he didn't want to hear something going on around him, he went into neutral by putting on headphones and snapping his fingers. When he chose not to hear me, I made sure to be in his face, at which point he would slide back into the groove of his music like a coward.

I thought I had seen it all at the age of fifteen. Hell, I was convinced I knew it all! I'd laid down the rules in my mother's house a year earlier—I'm my own person and I do not answer to anyone—and she abided by them. No one could tell me how to live my life, especially not him, but he adamantly pressed on whenever he got a chance.

The rules my father demanded I follow fell on deaf ears. When my brother and I spent a weekend at Dad's apartment, he'd curfew me at the ridiculous hour of eight o'clock. At the same time, he inappropriately admonished me to "watch out for guys that want to sleep with you—they may have diseases." In his worldview, guys were just a bunch of predators trying to get into a girl's panties. He convinced me it was true because a) my mother told me about *his* exploits, b) he talked to me about his sexual exploits, and c) Mom's friend had played the "train game" with me as a child. In some ways, he was as strict as a military general. Yet it made no sense. If he had graduated from West Point, then at least he would've had training and an ideology to follow. Dad's thinking was all about himself. "Do what I say, not what I do."

Little did he know that my group of friends and I had been sexually active for a year. In fact, he knew very little about my life except what I was willing to share, which wasn't much (I

Chapter 6 - Fucking My Way Through Europe

was more interested in cross-examining him about his ruthless behavior toward my Mom).

What era did this man live in, anyway? On the one hand, he appeared hip and with it because of his loose attitude toward his sexuality. He was super demonstrative in his affections and would often "feel up" his wife in front of my brother and me. That was fine by him because he rationalized he was just kibitzing. Yeah, sure, Dad!

On the other hand, he was controlling and unable to free himself from the time warp he inhabited—the late 1940s. It's as if he'd stopped progressing and growing when he reached his late teens. If I disagreed with him on anything, no matter how insignificant or weighty, he'd fly into a frenzied tantrum. It was shocking to witness since he had never ever shown that side of himself in all my years growing up with him in the same house. Even more shocking were the stories of his weird behavior that he relished telling.

"Did I tell you about the time I was driving on the beach and had to take a dump?"

"Um, no, and I have no desire to know more...."

But he would hammer on. "Well, there were no bathrooms, so I got out of the car and took a shit in the parking lot!" He was in hysterics over this grossly inappropriate act.

Even though it was the era of glam rock, prog rock, white-collar drugs, free sex and orgies, experimental art and lifestyles, and the breakup of the Beatles, you couldn't convince my Dad he was living in the seventies, despite his long, Engelbert Humperdinck sideburns and Jordache look. Looks deceived. It was a lesson that would plague me for years to come.

The summer of 1973 loomed, and if I didn't get away and do something positively savage, daring, and possibly deranged, all of Daddy's fears might come true. And worse.

My recurring nightmare from the time I moved to Long Island was becoming mediocre like the neighbors—of being a bore and having the unfathomable urge to keep up with the Joneses. Just thinking about life as a bourgeois suburbanite made me want to puke. The wealthier Jewish population called such types "JAPS"—Jewish American Princesses. I was NOT amongst them. Luckily my own parents were not role models for this type. I rebelled against conformism to such a degree as to sometimes endanger my own life.

So when my stepmom Rachel asked me one bright April afternoon what I'd prefer, a Sweet Sixteen party or a two-month trip to Europe, what do you think I chose?

Rachel and Dad cut out an advertisement from the Sunday *New York Times* magazine supplement and showed it to me. I almost fainted with excitement. I had only ever dreamed of going abroad, and here they were, presenting me with an unbelievable opportunity to travel to nine countries and numerous cities. I was totally down with that. The tour included stops in Amsterdam; the Netherlands; Bruges, Belgium; Luxembourg; Paris, Bordeaux, Avignon, and St. Tropez in France; Pisa, Rome, Positano, and Venice in Italy; Copenhagen, Denmark; Dresden, East Germany; Prague, Czechoslovakia; and Salzburg and Vienna in Austria.

This single gesture almost erased the ill feelings I harbored toward my father. He seemed to have proven his mettle.

Chapter 6 - Fucking My Way Through Europe

My stepmom made it clear that her eyes were wide open. It was her idea, after all. She was out-of-sight, unlike Dad (wink, wink)! Rachel was attuned to adventure. What struck my stepmom as unique was the unconventionality of the tour I was about to embark upon.

Teen tours—to Europe and throughout America—were all the rage that summer. I was the only one amongst my friends going to Europe, and I unabashedly told anyone passing me in the school hallways that I was going to get some culture, something those yahoo hicks definitely didn't have. I was thrilled.

I'd come back to show off the latest fashions, two years ahead of everyone else. Not that I had to, as I was already way ahead with my idiosyncratic attire without even having traveled overseas. After Europe, I'd be wearing black velvet secondhand dresses from the 1940s with a pillbox hat and platform shoes, the likes of which Roxy wore in silver glitter. Or I'd traipse into high school with a halter top and silk-striped pink and baby-blue bell-bottoms.

Coming back from Europe, I'd brag about how I'd tasted the best cheeses in France while those schlemiels were eating Kraft American plastic slices, or how I'd drunk the best wine and met European (*ooh-la-la*) men. I knew I'd leave a teenager and come back as a woman. I couldn't wait to be treated with the class and style lacking amongst my peers. My goal as a teen was to get over being a teenager as quickly as possible and grow up.

The anger at my father that I thought had subsided into nowhere resurged a few days before taking off to Europe. He refused to send me off at the airport because I hadn't visited him the weekend prior. What a big fat baby of a Dad I had! Instead, my Mom, brother, Grandpa Irving, and his new wife, Florence, gave me the send-off. I felt bad not seeing my stepsister before leaving on my trip. I adored her positive spirit and inquisitiveness. At six years old I relished being her older sis. She was the highlight of my visits to my Dad's home.

An intimate group of ten teens, ages sixteen to twenty, met at JFK airport in New York City. We were flying as unaccompanied minors (most of us) to Amsterdam, where the tour kicked off and where we'd meet our Dutch tour leader, Titus. From there, he'd drive us in a 1969 VW van throughout Europe. In each country, we'd camp out at sites located close to the city centers. Camping equipment was provided for the seven-week journey.

The only time I'd flown in an aircraft before this was in 1971 to Florida for the ritual spring break, and that was a piddly three-hour flight. This would take a good eight hours. The first person I befriended was Fiona Goldstein, who was my age. We sat next to each other on the plane. Yakety-yakking, I learned a lot about her: She came from a wealthy upper-middle-class Connecticut family who was Jewish yet disdained their own religion. She was raised Protestant, and I found that very disturbing. Was her family ashamed of their background? Overlooking that, I took an immediate liking to her, ingratiating myself to the girl who would be my touring buddy and my student of life.

She wore her long flowing chestnut hair pulled back into a hot cross bun. Her Semitic features sans the freckles were darkly mysterious, and her eyes were mischievous. She was sixteen like me but hid her womanly body beneath the universal dress code

Chapter 6 - Fucking My Way Through Europe

of the day—wide flares and an equally full bell-sleeved cotton hippie shirt in a nonsensical batik print—whereas I flaunted my wares with short fringed vests with nothing underneath them. Her statement piece was a headband made of cow leather.

Fiona confessed to me that she'd never made love, probably because at the all-girls' boarding schools she attended, the teachers were strict. When we met, she'd been tucked away in Puget Sound, Washington State, far away from her family—like across-the-continent far.

I greatly appreciated her intellectual prowess and extensive vocabulary, which reminded me of Miche. Verbose, she spoke French, which impressed me terribly, if only because I adored Edith Piaf and Jacques Brel. I found the French language ultra-cool—totally affected and presumptuous. Maybe I was arrogant in the way I thought I was imitating the cadence?

Fiona first appeared prudish around the boys we met. Perhaps it was charming to them? She hadn't been exposed to the sex, drugs, and rock 'n' roll of the seventies that was now unfolding before her eyes. Lorenzo Bianco was the only male in our group of ten touring teens and the eldest at twenty. An architect and amateur photographer, his physique was swarthy, muscular, and stocky, yet attractive. Shy yet flirtatious, a loner with an effortless communicative style, Lorenzo was the watchdog of the troupe. The rest were utterly provincial, so I ignored them the entire two months. One girl was brainwashed into performing TM—transcendental meditation—every day, anywhere, at least five times a day.

Fiona and I would sing, "In the a.m. and the p.m. do your

TM, do your TM, but don't forget to brush your teeth so you can have a transcen-dental experience."

I understood why Fiona looked up to me. I had both common sense and mature experiences—at least that's what I led her to believe. What I had, in fact, was no shame or inhibitions, nor condemnation toward sexuality or my gender. I felt like a hermaphrodite: aggressive/determined male mind-set and a sexy feminine physique. This conflicted me terribly. Emotionally I was a super-sensitive romantic idealist. The exterior was like the Israeli saber: tough and sharp. I related emotionally to Ayn Rand's main character Howard, a supreme individualist in *The Fountainhead*.

Fiona and I agreed on my definition of types of humans: leaders, followers, and individualists. She joined my imaginary club of the latter. Together we set the policy for our club and rites of initiation, self-imposed no less. We both felt extraordinarily powerful in our self-restraint and in our ability to limit ourselves to our own conventions.

We established a ritual in Belgium to serve our sexual fantasies and experiences marvelously on our trip. First, pitch the tent, change clothes into something sheer, brush our teeth and wash up; then go to the campsite bar and begin scouting.

Step two: Never order a drink. Wait until the guys we wanted took notice of us, then flirt with them until they offered to buy us a beer. Within the hour, we were sure to find a solid catch, one or more for both of us.

Our trip through Europe was not so much a cultural, historical, or artistic journey through ancient civilizations as it was

Chapter 6 - Fucking My Way Through Europe

a scientific comparison of national cocks, bedding techniques, and mannerisms before, during, and after the act of copulation. My primary source of transportation was humping. We imagined ourselves as Attila the Hun attacking Constantinople, leaving a trail of burnt-out men along our path.

To the Winner Go the Spoils 1973
Here's a rundown of our spoils.

Amsterdam, The Netherlands: We were in Vondel Park, a miniature version of Central Park, located in the center of the city near the hopping and bopping Leidseplein, where you could smoke pot in the cafés by day and dance at the Paradiso disco by night.

We laid out a blanket to smoke grass and hashish in the open air since it was legal. People slept on the grass, and some were nude; others made love under a gazebo. Three guys, Gerrit, Hans, and Jan, strolled by and invited themselves to our blanket. We didn't refuse. They were very laid-back.

We rolled around on the damp grass, all of us entangled in some strange Dutch casserole. Who knows who did what to whom? Did we care? Fiona and I noticed, however, that two of them were masturbating. We found this offensive.

"Why do they need to do it themselves when we're here?" I commented to Fiona. "I've seen a lot of people dance by themselves looking straight into the mirrors at the discos and clubs in the city, but this is going too far." I felt uncomfortable and wanted to leave them to their own devices.

"Let's stay for a while and see what happens," she leaned

over and whispered in my ear between puffs of a Dutch spliff. The Dutch rolled their marijuana with tobacco into a cone shape and vigorously inhaled as if it were a bong. What was there to find out? These narcissists were into themselves, not us.

I have no idea what happened after inhaling one or two puffs from that impressive joint Fiona had. I might have fallen asleep. We walked around the park with the three guys until we found something to eat at a kiosk. The boys explained that eating a *broodje tartar* (a sandwich of raw chopped beef) with freshly chopped onions sprinkled on top was very Dutch and we ought to try it, so we did.

Bruges, Belgium: Fiona and I had dropped some acid, and for her, it was the very first time. We hallucinated to the light show at the local church. Live music of Mussorgsky's "Pictures at an Exhibition" was performed, and I mistook it for Emerson, Lake & Palmer's version. Fiona met two inconspicuous-looking fellows and we followed them into town after the performance. They offered to buy us french fries wrapped in a newsprint cone, with a two-pronged plastic fork, for dinner. There were mounds of mayonnaise on the fries because Belgians don't eat them with ketchup. I thought it was gross. I hated it, and besides, it was such a goyim thing, like mayo on white bread with bologna. Ick!

The two boys both had shoulder-length dark brown hair. I chose the one whose facial hairs look softer. I disliked beards and mustaches; they're unkempt and scratchy. In fact, I wasn't too fond of body hair either. Boys with hair on their back and chest totally turned me off. I preferred a more androgynous look and feel.

Chapter 6 - Fucking My Way Through Europe

My guy, Jacques, was around two meters tall. I was talking in meters and liters, and not to be cool or anything. I just wanted to be intelligent if I went into a shop to buy something. The metric system made perfect sense to me, a non-mathematical student. I could visualize metrics and spatially had no problem understanding what a meter was, compared with inches and yards and miles. I didn't have a clue what those meant spatially!

I was trying to figure out how long Jacques' cock was in centimeters. "Fiona, how long is your guy's thing in centimeters?" I asked while she was humping him against a brick wall. She shrugged, totally uninterested in my question.

I started what I think was a measurement system, putting my thumb and pointer finger in a backward C shape near his dick. He cracked up laughing, totally not offended.

Jacques smelled like *pommes frites* and tar. We continued making love to these strangers in the alleyway around the corner from the place where we got the fries. No one was around. We could hear our own breathing.

When we finally returned to the campsite, it was almost sunrise. We discovered mayonnaise drippings all over our bodies. The acid was wearing off, though. We thought the mayo was a Peter Max psychedelic painting. Laughing our heads off, we took hot showers before Titus could notice anything suspicious.

Paris, France: Fiona and I had a slew of followers. Two Germans followed Fiona (both could speak French) into town on Bastille Day while I remained at the campsite. A group of Dutchmen, five in all, invited me to eat with them. Edo Hartman is who I fell for. Over two meters tall, slinky with gorgeous curly shoulder-length hair, almond-shaped sunken blue eyes, and thick eyebrows, he boldly introduced himself and his gang. He staked his claim. I was his girl.

He was provocatively shy yet flirty and giggled a lot. He and his crew all spoke pretty decent English. We discovered that mostly every Dutch person was fluent in three or more languages: English, German, and perhaps French. Those Dutchies were the most versatile of the Europeans we'd met thus far, with a cavalier attitude.

Edo was twenty-one and a sportswriter with the Amsterdam-based *Telegraph* daily newspaper. The only spectator sport I wanted to participate in with him was fornication. He had other designs. He fell in love with me and, out of a sense of honor and dignity, refused to make love. He wanted to pet only. He probably weighed in at less than one hundred and sixty pounds (I still hadn't gotten down the kilos-to-pounds conversion, but I was working on that). He smelled like dark roasted coffee and grass, probably because he drank a ton of the stuff as most Dutchies did, even as teenagers. For that matter, they were allowed to drink beer from sixteen on, yet they seemed to be the sanest of everyone.

Later on, I met up with Fiona. She told me that she "frenched with the Krauts" in a café near La Pousse—the flea market on the outskirts of Paris. She gave double blow jobs simultaneously in an empty Metro car to both guys.

Excited to share her ventures, she divulged, "They each touched a titty in public and kept their hands secured to my breasts. They kept telling me how charming I was, whispering, '*Je*

Chapter 6 - Fucking My Way Through Europe

t'aime.' It didn't impress me, Elise." She wagged her finger, acting all French and snooty. That said, the size of her little mouth did impress them.

Avignon, France: At the foothills of the walled city, Fiona met a Frenchman with a beret. How quaint. By this time, she had shed whatever insecurities she'd acquired in America. They went immediately to the tent and started fucking on my mattress. I was pissed. I stormed away in a tizzy and went to wash up, and then I heard, "Yoo-hoo, Elise, I followed you. Surprise, it's Edo."

My heart rushed with the good type of adrenaline. Edo and I spent a quiet evening alone in the city drinking white wine and eating fish at the port. He taught me how to cut and fillet a fish with a knife properly. We kissed for what seemed like hours on end. After dinner I sat on his lap and we cuddled at the restaurant; he teased me that we'd be together forever and have twenty-two children. That became our inside joke.

St. Tropez, France: Were we impressed with this town? Not at all. What was the hullabaloo all about? A little strip of sand, a port town that doesn't compare with teeny-weeny Greenwich, Connecticut. Huh? We didn't get what the fuss was all about. We didn't try to meet anyone probably because there was no bar at the campsite. It was the worst campsite we'd been to thus far. Titus, our tour guide, said it was probably because rich people don't go to campgrounds. He had a point. Edo and gang followed us again and invited us for an aperitif at the harbor. Nothing of interest happened to Fiona, but I could feel I was falling in love with Edo. This love was magnified by the distance I was from America. It had been thousands of miles since I was in love with

Joshua, but that was only two years earlier. I felt as if I'd been thousands of miles away from any genuine love my whole life.

Marseilles, France: Edo and the gang followed us again, arriving earlier than us, so we didn't have any time to pitch the tent because they wanted to roam the town. They dragged us to the port, acting as our tour guides. Willem, a dark-haired friend who rolled his own tobacco (which stank like a skunk), was smitten with Fiona. He had been part of Edo's gang from the get-go, yet until Marseilles, he didn't make a move on her.

She was aloof yet managed to squeeze in a few competent French kisses while squeezing his butt in front of us. Edo fondled me whenever we were alone, whether in a church, visiting architectural wonders, or on a side street. I caressed back, always teasing that I'd rip off his clothes and take a good bite. For the first time, we slept together in my tent with our clothes on, embracing and touching ever so thoughtfully. His caresses were like gentle waves of light. I'd never felt this way before.

Lauterbrunnen, Switzerland: Because my tour group was departing, Edo and I had to say farewell for a time, but we knew we'd be reuniting before I left Europe entirely. His gang was planning on staying in France.

I was glad to be alive and out of the magical mystery VW tour bus as Titus drove recklessly in the mountain passes without guardrails. I was screaming at him to slow down, and he just laughed. At over one hundred and twenty kilometers per hour, twisting and turning on those small roads wasn't at all amusing.

Fiona and I hiked up the Jungfrau, a thousand-plus-foot mountain, without hiking boots, and got to the top. What a

Chapter 6 - Fucking My Way Through Europe

fantastic vista of the jagged snowcapped mountain range and the leprechaun-green valley below. In the little inn, we ordered a liter of beer apiece and a melted Swiss cheese and ham sandwich. Beat and Marcus, both with thick blondish-brown lion's manes, blue eyes, masculine builds, and not an ounce of flab, looked like twins. Giggling, they delighted in their flirtatiousness with us.

Don't ask how we ever communicated with them. Both these boys couldn't understand a word of English, Fiona's French didn't work on them, and my seventh-grade Spanish was for naught. We took a cable car down the mountain with the two laughing cats. Beat pointed to a clock tower. With hand rotations and finger language, we worked out that we'd meet that evening by the tower at nine o'clock.

That evening, Beat and Marcus were dressed to kill. Pressed jeans and ironed T-shirts exposed their girth. I don't recall having seen anyone in ironed jeans before, but it was suave. We walked with them into the forest valley, where they produced some Swiss wine, thick bread, and Emmentaler cheese. Who knew the Swiss even produced wine? We didn't. Fiona and I deduced that this was going to be more than just a night picnic.

After a few swigs of wine and bites of bread, Fiona and I winked as if on cue. Then we attacked these farm boys by ripping off their clothes, jumping on their bones, then riding them as if they were horses, while we held the reins. Fiona and I led the way while the boys just laughed.

They were so virile and virginal that they came not more than fifteen seconds after we mounted them. It was hardly enough time for the cheering section at the horse race to clamor for a good look-see. We did not get our money's worth. Fiona blew her toy whistle as if to shriek "foul play." She then shrugged and directed me to take the wine and cheese.

Just as we were ready to split, the boys reversed roles and showed us what mountain males can do. They pushed us to the ground like the studs they were pretending to be. As we shouted in orgasmic pleasure (it was a first for us!), both our bushes were sprayed with their pristine mineral tongues, our vocal cords competing for basso and treble. As I came, I sputtered, "I'm a Jungfrau, a Virgo on the verge of ex-virginity." Awash in feminine ecstasy, I heard cowbells.

Fiona chuckled, then zipped her pants perfunctorily. Beat hurriedly scribbled in squirrel-like handwriting his vital statistics as we waved goodbye. There was sadness in his eyes as he handed me his address. He picked a few mountain flowers and threw them in my direction. Ah, life is but a dream.

Rome, Italy: Fiona kept a diary of how many men we had, where they were from, and the number of languages they could speak. We cross-referenced the countries we visited with the nationalities we devoured. Thus far, Fiona hadn't had a German or Italian. I hadn't had a Frenchman or a German.

At the campsite, we had an overflowing choice of men. Rome was probably the hottest spot of all. I had an Italian who was twenty-five and spoke sixteen languages. He was a scholar and pitifully dull. Industriously quizzing me with "Do you understand, *capece, comprende, verstehen Sie, begrijp je, wakarimasu ka?*" and so on, his hands lingered too long in one spot, spoiling the mood. I asked him, "*Vaffanculo,* Capece?" then shooed him out of the tent.

Chapter 6 - Fucking My Way Through Europe

We were hot teenagers, our bodies streaming with hormonal juices, our senses challenged by the mere sight of someone with perfectly shaped buttocks or a handheld-size hard tool. I liked the taller specimens and preferred a dark mane. Blondes never really did it for me.

Before leaving for Venice, I met a German: Gunther from Hamburg. We jumped into the Trevi fountain together and got our legs wet. He was throwing the pennies and coins that the tourists wished upon back out to them, and I was playing along.

I toyed with his burgeoning vanity like a puppeteer teasing him into uncompromising positions. He wouldn't let me put my fingers where they wanted to travel. I was his pulsating heart-throb even though I acted snobby, aloof, and not too pleased with the size of his baby wee. He was sensitive and felt soft, with long lashes and bedroom eyes. We exchanged phone numbers.

Nothing happened in Venice because Fiona and I decided not to go farther than St. Mark's Square. After witnessing thousands of pigeons anointing innocent bystanders with holy pellets of poop, we chose to spend our days on Lido Beach playing table football with enthusiastic youngsters.

Prague, Czechoslovakia (Plague): We were ridiculed in a pub by coal workers who taunted us with crude drawings of the devil. They insulted us by calling out *"Diablo Americano"* and pointing their stubby fingers in our direction. Fiona was better with illustration than me; I was the wordsmith. She drew a crude picture of a hammer and sickle with a bleeding heart and shoved that in their fat faces. They didn't intimidate us. We ordered Pilsner Urquell beer from the tap and munched on some deep-fried cheese sticks.

Plague was also the place where we altruistically donated our Marlboros and jeans to a group of theatrical performers who strummed Grace Slick's anti-American ballad on their guitars under the clocktower. In exchange for these hard-to-get items, they loaded us with worthless paper zloty. We went into a communist supermarket. Eerily empty, and stocking what could've been a precursor to no-brand labels, the shelves had barely anything worth buying. We couldn't give that money away, except when we left the country, where the authorities took it all upon departure. Hard currency wasn't allowed out of the country.

Dresden, Germany (Depressden): This was a case of depression and misery. No boys to meet anywhere, probably because we were only passing through on our way to Austria. We stopped at a government-run restaurant in a coal-smeared brick house on a dirt road. The enormous X-shaped metal barriers and barbed wire strung along forgotten train tracks (which had probably been used to transfer Jews to the concentration camps, I thought) gave it an ominous feel. The sky was a bleak gray, and the concrete blocks lining the city were dressed in the uniform of communist conformity. It was just like the public housing projects in the Bronx that were burning or already burnt to the ground. Now I understood why the U.S. did that, or why the Communist East imitated the West in this regard. The immoral practice of herding people like nameless cattle into such housing developments robbed them of all individuality and dignity. That's the true purpose: to keep Blacks and Puerto Ricans or other underserved populations controlled by the government. Tell me, is there any difference between what America does with its poor

Chapter 6 - Fucking My Way Through Europe

and what authoritarian countries like East Germany did? Yeah, perhaps one difference: In Eastern Europe there was free health care, free rent, and jobs for all, even if those jobs (as I learned from Titus) were not what the individual studied for or chose. Still, the realization that we Americans actively suppressed non-whites using psychological warfare enraged me. What got me even more riled up was the sickening attitudes of whites (my father included, bigot that he was) who believed "Blacks don't want to work; they're lazy" sort of racist bullshit. A masculine though very overweight matron in a drab beige 1960s house dress style thing came out behind the kitchen wearing an angry scowl.

There were no menus of course, no choice. You get what you are served, more like you get what is available that week. We were served in beige plastic bowls and plates what consisted of some mushy potatoes, pickles, and mystery meat in the color of spam gone bad. We couldn't eat it. I skipped to the bathroom as my stomach was turning. Inside the filthy stall was a turn-of-the-century metal chain with a ball at its end that, when pulled, released water into the tank above the toilet. That's why in Europe the bathroom was called a WC (water closet) and not a bathroom, since no one took a proper bath in the room where you peed and shat.

Salzburg, Austria (Salt Mines): We pitched our tents and then went with the entire group to the salt mines after dropping by Mozart's birth house. Wearing white uniforms, we ventured into the tunnel riding an open-air bus, the kind you see at zoos or amusement parks. Afterward, in town, we ate tasty pastries like the famous Linzer torte, then took a stroll along the Danube. The river was dotted with ivy geraniums and was not exactly blue like the waltz, yet it was truly one of the more magnificent sights in Europe. Fiona and I lamented our lack.

I began to miss Edo, yet I saw no contradiction in my quest for new men of prey. If boys sowed their oats before they settled down, I certainly was entitled to. And since I wasn't planning on *ever* settling down, I fully permitted myself to indulge in hedonistic pleasures.

Fiona and I had a long conversation on the banks of the Danube. "The type of relationship I want is like what George Sand and Chopin, or Lillian Hellman and Dashiel Hammet, had. Living together sometimes, yet constantly maintaining a love-friendship. Ideally, I could see myself having my own flat, and him having his, and us sharing our time together. Because I need my space, my freedom to come and go as I please and to discover whatever," I confided to her.

She chimed in, "I don't like American guys at all; they're macho and abrasive, always trying to prove who's a 'man,' and it's all because the women are still playing girlie games—a bunch of Barbie dictators competing for boys and prettying themselves up to show other girls down."

I fully agreed with her. My stomach churned with righteous indignation because this way of separating boys from girls caused war between the sexes. "Did you know there are three sexes?" I inquired.

"Of course—heteros, gays, and others," she replied.

"I believe that we all have male and female aspects in us, so when the scales are tipped too much to an extreme, I get into

Chapter 6 - Fucking My Way Through Europe

conflicts with those kinds of people. It winds up that the men I like are the ones who are sensitive, showing their feminine side. They're not trying to control me. They're not telling me what to do, how to do it, and when to do what. What's your kind of relationship look like, Fiona?"

"I don't want to get married," she said. "I'd rather live with someone without the institutionalization, and I don't want to have children. It's not my biological duty to produce kids; there are enough of them in the world today. The planet is already overpopulated, starving, and underprivileged.

"I want a man who basically has an intellect equal to mine, someone with whom I can have long conversations about anything—from Marxism to the crisis of migrant workers in America. I don't care what country he's from, but he wouldn't be another race."

"Why not?" I provoked her. "Are you prejudiced, or is it just that your parents would take away your privileges?"

Skirting the issue, she tossed her head back and waved her hand in the air as if to brush the topic away. "There's enough strife in the world as it is, and I see no reason to add to it."

We shook hands and agreed that marriage is definitely out, living together is in, abortion is our own choice, and having babies is not what we have to do, as liberated females.

Copenhagen, Denmark: Tivoli Gardens is one of the main features in the capital. It reminded me of the rides on Coney Island, only far more glamorous and squeaky shiny. The park is in the center of the city overlooking the port where the famed bronze sculpture by Edvard Eriksen sits atop a rock of The Little Mermaid.

It was near the port that Fiona and I met two boys. One had crazy wavy hair that looked like a white boy's Afro, the other boy looked like a typical Dane with straight bangs of dirty blond hair cut in a later day Beatles style, big blue eyes and a friendly demeanor. We walked along the port then entered a coffee shop in a small timber house painted Swedish red that looked like a cross between a Tudor home with Mediterranean roof tiles in sienna. Lined against the window ledges were flowerpots of lilacs bursting with color against the simple white interior. It was fresh and sunny.

One of the boys invited us to his parent's home a bit outside the city. We rode bicycles - I think they were borrowed (or stolen?) near the coffee shop. Twenty five minutes later we were being served home-made raspberry jam on hard rusk bread by a jovial Danish mom whose English was impeccable.

Each of us took a boy. I chose the wild looking one and all four of us proceeded to clomp up the stairs to a bedroom where we made out for quite a while. The mom encouraged us too, waving us in the direction of the steps with a friendly smile and a twinkle in her eyes as if to say have fun kids and see you later kids. As dusk was upon us Fiona and I needed to get back to Tivoli where we were supposed to be the whole day, otherwise we would be in big trouble. We hurried out and rode the bikes back to the center. Both boys gave us their addresses and phone numbers and promised to be in touch.

Amsterdam, The Netherlands: We headed back to Amsterdam for only two days before leaving for our respective homes in America. On the second and last day, Edo and I planned to

Chapter 6 - Fucking My Way Through Europe

see each other. He wanted to introduce me to his parents, which touched me deeply. I thought the introduction meant he was serious about me, about us as a thing. I was distraught over leaving him.

He lived within a three-minute walk of the famous Vondel Park, where this dream of a trip all began seven weeks earlier. On the Stadhouderskade street, the attached homes had tall, narrow staircases that seemed to be vertical and that could, if you weren't careful, be the cause of your death.

Edo showed me how to walk sideways as if I were skiing, but that was a weak reference, as I had skied only once and therefore had no solid knowledge of how to use skis. Inside, we went straight to the kitchen. His parents were lovely people who invited me to sit and sip coffee together. The tablecloth and window dressings were made of white doilies, spun from cotton in the eighteenth century. How quaint, just like Holland, I thought.

After coffee and biscuits, we went to Edo's bedroom, where I cried my eyes out in his tender, long arms that seemed to wrap around me twice. He lifted my chin and reminded me there's nothing to be sad about since we'll be having twenty-two children together. I felt as if I were Queen Esther to Edo's Mordechai, with one exception: I wasn't celebrating my release. We caressed and kissed for several hours. Before I left, he gave me two beautiful presents: a dainty porcelain coffee cup and tray adorned with orange and yellow daffodils, and a silver bracelet filled with amber stones.

Edo promised to write me love letters so our summer romance would linger just a little longer. It was devastating to leave him, and I didn't want to part or go back to America or school or anything at all. I clung to him on the street as we gave each other our last hugs goodbye. At dusk, the VW van stopped in front of his apartment to whisk me away from my love forever. I cried all the way to Schiphol airport, even onto the tarmac.

As I was ascending the stairs of the aircraft, I heard my name being called—more like howled—in the wind of the turbines. My Edo was throwing daffodils onto the tarmac, blowing kisses to me and waving goodbye. My heart totally melted; my eyes filled with more tears than I could bear. And that is how I left Europe.

Photos

Where I lived from birth to 5 years old in the Bronx

PS 99 - My elementary school

Photos

Lillian and her daughter Stephonic, Richard, Mom and me 1968

Me and Richard in Florida 1972

Europe with Edo and friends 1973

Gunther's mom & sis, Hamburg, Germany 1974

Photos

My first apartment in NYC 1976

KISS press kit cover

MEMO FROM
Alvin S. Ross

ARRANGEMENTS FOR TODAY (20) AND TOMORROW.

1- There will be <u>no</u> dinner this evening. The planned dinner with the group will be held in one of the other cities.

2- Don't forget, bags should be outside your doors at 11:30 AM.

3- I have arranged private cars to take all the press people to the Hilton Hotel tomorrow for the Press Conference. Please gather at the third floor elevators at 12:20 PM.

4- At the conclusion of the press conference you will be joining the Victor Record Co. people for lunch.

5- At 5:00 PM the cars will leave for the airport from the Hilton Hotel.

6- When we arrive in OSAKA, there will be a bus to take us to the hotel.

KISS Japan tour memo

Japan concert 1977

Chapter 7 - A Nazi Son's Revenge

Flushing, Queens & Hamburg, Germany 1974

I proudly accomplished the two goals I had set for myself: graduating high school one year early in 1974 and quitting pot. As a fair-to-middling student in all subjects except English, poetry, and study hall, where I achieved A-level status, I had little to no patience for boring lectures on topics I had no interest in or subjects I felt had no practical value (such as high-level mathematics). That would later come to haunt me as I matured. Not the mathematics part, but the arrogant part, where if I deemed something or someone else's opinion "less important" than my own, I would totally ignore it and pretend it didn't exist.

Nor was I thrilled about a future of four years of college. All I could think about was Europe. I desperately wanted to live there or, at the very least, get a full-time job at home so I could return as quickly as possible. I wasn't thoroughly convinced of that idea, though. I didn't want to be at home. What to do?

As kismet would have it, I received an international telephone call: surprise surprise, Gunther calling from Germany. We had met the previous summer in Rome on my European trip, and he wanted to try his luck and take the plunge of living on his own for the very first time. In New York!

Although he wasn't on my list of "top ten" summer loves, I

certainly did remember him. And it dawned on me that perhaps, just maybe, I could get back to Europe with him. Not that Germany was a place I had any intention of visiting. Our tour guide, Titus, had avoided it the previous year, except for Dresden. I learned later that most Dutch reviled the Germans (even though the Dutch willingly handed over the most Jews per capita to the SS, compared with every other nation that was invaded during WWII).

Once Gunther arrived, Mom kindly offered to help him find an apartment in Flushing, Queens, which was not exactly around the corner from where I was in the sticks on Long Island. It was also quite generous of her to drive him around, because we were still caught up in the oil crisis of the previous December in 1973. Massive stretches of automobiles were lined up on side streets, at gas stations, near train stations, on highways, and through neighborhoods, waiting for a turn at the gas pump. Sometimes we'd be in line at the Sunoco station for two hours! But when my mother liked someone, she would put on her bells and whistles and go all out for them. She did enjoy Gunther.

An apartment in Flushing was all he could afford, and it was close enough to get into the city on the number 7 train. We took him shopping for a mattress and some basics, as the apartment we found was furnished. His great adventure ended in less than a month. He was homesick and felt bewildered to find himself in a foreign country within a foreign country. Flushing was, at the time, an enclave of Taiwanese and Koreans, interspersed with a growing Japanese community and non-Hispanic whites.

Mom took him back to our house so he could think about his

Chapter 7 - A Nazi Son's Revenge

next steps. Gunther was madly in love with me and wanted me to return with him to Hamburg, to his family. Not to marry me, he said—but who knew what his real motivation was? I saw his affectionate overture as my grand opportunity to get back to the continent I knew I belonged in, so I agreed to go back with him to Germany.

Of course I was attracted to him, but not to the depths of love that he felt for me. I found his personality to be pleasantly receptive, noncombative, and accommodating. His longish brown hair, soft and wispy, was parted in the middle and swayed to his footsteps. There was an angelic quality to him, not unlike the whitewashed images of Jesus. His tender, oceanic eyes framed the longest eyelashes I had ever seen and were dangerously inviting.

First, though, he had to determine whether to phone his father. He needed to get permission for me to come back with him from his dad, a former Nazi! "Absolutely not" was the first response. His dad hung up the phone on him. Although his father was adamantly against the idea, his mother was aghast at her husband's declarations of post-national socialist racism. Gunther was appalled and distraught, even though he knew better.

Eventually, his mother's sentiments of guilt won out, and I was given the green light. My mother was ever ready and keen to let me fly to far-flung locations. I appreciated her reluctantly. She was ungenerous in so many ways yet when it came to the pursuit of freedom via travel I was permitted to spread my metaphorical wings. Maybe she allowed me this space to compensate for her envy. Her emotional responses to travel were without borders. To make up for her nonexistent international travel, she allowed me to take risks that, in a sense, I was unprepared for.

Until that summer, I'd never worn a Jewish Star of David around my neck. Yet before embarking for the Fatherland, I bought the biggest in-your-face star I could find. It was white, made of faux ivory, approximately three inches in diameter, and hung on a silver chain. I put it around my neck, determined not to take it off as long as I walked the blood-soaked pavement in that northern city. That's where Hitler's willing participants existed, I reminded myself. And there was a huge concrete bunker in Hamburg I recalled from the books I'd read about the Holocaust.

At the time, the German people were still reeling from the war and many were in denial. Gunther's friends and the younger generation hadn't yet been exposed in school to the real horrors committed by the Gestapo. While Gunther was in New York, I basically made him watch a PBS WWII documentary, which explicitly showed some of the inhumane experiments perpetrated upon the Jewish people. Gunther was mortified. He wept uncontrollably for hours at the sight of the tormented souls he saw on the black-and-white TV screen. I consoled him on the one hand but also reacted quite aggressively. I ranted about the idiocy of denial, going on and on about the hypocritical German system. How could they dismiss the truth about what happened? How could students ever learn not to repeat the sins of their elders? What did he actually think took place?

The Gass family resided in a McMansion-style corner home in one of Hamburg's leafier, more affluent areas near the Elbchaussee, known for its stately homes and villas. Although it felt and looked like suburbia, it was still within the Hamburg city limits. It took Gunther and me around fifteen minutes by bus

Chapter 7 - A Nazi Son's Revenge

to get downtown to the Big Alster Lake where the discos were. Sometimes we would take the U-Bahn (subway). Each time I knew we'd be taking the bus, though, I would hurriedly put on that Jewish star to shock those Nazi geezers sitting properly on the bus.

You should've seen the looks on their faces. I'm talking about an older-than-fifty crowd who rode that particular bus, number 47. Shock. Embarrassment. Guilt. Yet no remorse, redness, or extreme discomfort ran across their faces. Not a single one of them could look at me, but I certainly looked at them, staring right into their eyeballs. I flaunted the fact that *I was alive.* And how did they like that? Hmpf. A survivor in their wake, riding their bus, in their 'hood, walking with pride.

The homes in his neighborhood were inhabited by old monied folk. I imagined that those homes were stolen from Jewish merchants and professionals during the 1930s. Everywhere I looked, there were Mercedes and BMWs lining the driveways. People dressed appropriately, almost too formal. The elderly ladies wore blouses under cardigans or scoop-neck woolen sweaters, with long plaid skirts that touched their calves.

There was a sizable geriatric population. I didn't see many men or young people on the streets. The sidewalks were predictably spotless, and not one shrub appeared to be out of place. They seemed to be monitored by a force of nature that employed Edward Scissorhands.

Gunther warned me about his father's stoicism and curmudgeonly attitude. I decided to play the role of a provocateur in his presence. I wasn't afraid of him either. Literally, what was he going to do to me? Make a lampshade out of me? Herr Gass was a stout five-foot-nine-inch unfriendly fellow. His receding, curly hairline and angry countenance reminded me of Larry in the Three Stooges. He never once spoke to me except the very first time I stepped inside his home, and all he said was *"guten tag."* For the remainder of the time I lived there, he'd throw me nasty glances and purposely play 33 RPMs of Hitler's most cherished speeches. I was subjected to the Billboard Top 100 playlist of maniacal expressions by the Führer every single night when Gunther and I returned home from a day's adventure in town.

Mütter Gass reminded me so much of my beloved Grandma Faye it made me cry. It was uncanny. Except for her hair, which was longer, past her shoulders. Frau Gass's hair looked as if it could be used as a warm scarf in winter. Her blue eyes were gentle yet piercing. Don't all Germans, though, have blue eyes? That's what the entire deluded theory of the Aryan race was about—genetic superiority. Hitler didn't even have blue eyes, but I do. I mean, I am one-quarter German, after all.

One night while Herr Asshole was listening gleefully to his Hilter speeches, Gunther and I sat down on the flower-printed Victorian sofa next to him. He was drinking a pilsner with a little too much of his beer belly exposed. His squinty eyes and thin lips belied a lame intellect. He was a Nazi, after all, and in my opinion, they are all deformed. When you have no conscience and systematically destroy humans as if they are "things," that is a gross deformity.

Gunther didn't want to speak with him at all, ever, which is why we always went right up to his room on the second floor or

Chapter 7 - A Nazi Son's Revenge

scooted to the kitchen to visit his mother when we got home. In the mornings, we ate breakfast unattended. Gunter protected me at all costs.

I ventured to ask Herr Gass a series of questions through Gunther, who was my translator. We both had to increase the decibel of our voices way above the ranting lunacy of Hitler's to be heard. Gunther was relatively soft-spoken, unlike me. I could be as subtle as a sledgehammer.

"What did you do during the war?" I asked. "What was your job?" I pressed on. "Were you in the SS?" I demanded to know. "How many people did you murder?"

He muttered some nonsense to Gunther to avoid answering my questions. I continued, but that only angered him more. He refused to give me a response.

Gunther's mom tried to mitigate the situation by providing more beer to her husband and, to us, vanilla semolina pudding with fresh strawberries on top. It was the best pudding I'd ever eaten, but I refused to be bought out by treats. So I raised my voice even louder. *"What did you do during the war?"*

He jumped out of his seat and snarled, "I was a soldier then, and I'm a soldier now." Then stomped off to his study. Frau Gass shook. She didn't dare reprimand me because, after all, I was there in Hamburg thanks to her guilty conscience.

As the manager of Wurlitzer (makers of the jukebox, pinball, and other gaming machines) for northern Germany, Herr Gass would collect the coins from the hundreds of *kneiepe* (bars) throughout the region religiously every Friday. When he got home, he'd sit at the kitchen table and unload the coins into a money-sorting machine. Out they'd pop, all wrapped up in thick paper marked by denomination for Monday's bank deposit. Once they were checked for exact amounts, he'd stock them like the soldier he was in the living room wall unit, adjacent to the kitchen. There was nothing else in that wall unit save for the temporary coin collection.

After three months, I decided it was time to wave *auf wiedersehen* to Gunther. I made a few phone calls to friends in Amsterdam. The first one was to my big love of the previous summer, Edo. I missed him. I wished to be with him again but was broken-hearted when we actually spoke. He said that all the kisses and caresses, letters sent, and words spoken were just a summer's romance and nothing more. And please, do not visit him if I go to Amsterdam. Just forget all about him.

I manually dialed several other boys I met from Holland. Gerrit, the last one on my list, was gung-ho to meet again, although honestly, I had little recall of him. I guess he was just a one-night fuck whose address I had in my phone book. He was living with his mother in a two-bedroom flat in Amsterdam Oost (east side), and yes, I could stay with them.

I said my goodbyes to Gunther's mother and older sister. Gunther drove me to the central train station. Once we arrived, he went to look for a parking spot while I purchased my ticket; he promised to catch up with me at the café. When he returned, he was lugging a large, heavy-duty black suitcase. We drank a coffee then headed up to the platform. I told him I had all of my belongings and didn't leave anything extra at his house.

"Why on earth are you bringing this luggage?" I inquired.

Chapter 7 - A Nazi Son's Revenge

"It's for you, Elise. It's a going-away present. Open it when you get on the train," he said.

I cherished the consideration invested in thinking about what to give someone as a gift - both the giving and receiving were particularly humble acts I loved to partake in. I was excited to see what was inside. Gunther helped me with the baggage as I couldn't lug it onto the train by myself. We said our farewells and hugged each other tearfully. Then the train whistle blew, indicating he had to disembark; otherwise, he would be on his way to Amsterdam with me.

We waved as the train rolled out of the station. Like a film noir, the glass became misty until both of us were out of each other's sight. I opened the luggage and almost had a heart attack. Therein were hundreds of Deutsche Marks' worth of five-and ten-pfennig coins rolled into packets.

Gunther had stolen the money from his father's wall unit. Once I was settled in Amsterdam, I counted the coins so I could convert them into Dutch Guilders. He had gifted me over one thousand Deutsche Marks! In today's dollars, that would be equivalent to over three or four thousand U.S. dollars. It was the Nazi son's form of reparations.

Chapter 8 - I'm Gonna Be a Rock 'n' Roll Journalist

New York, NY 1975

During my senior year of high school, I had tangible help in recognizing the two innate talents of mine: writing and music, which I could combine to create what would become my dream job as a music journalist. I owe a debt of gratitude to my poetry teacher, Mr. Strumpf, an erstwhile moral ally, who not only encouraged me to pursue a career in writing but helped me to write my first pitch letter to magazines. He taught me how to sell myself. More crucially, he listened to me, unlike my mother, who constantly interrupted me while I read aloud my prose or poetry with stupid gossip like "did you hear about what so-and-so said," oblivious to how she hurt me with such dismissive trivialities.

Being in his class quelled my frivolous attitude toward education! He was my first real mentor, a model of rectitude and patience. I was encouraged to read my poetry and prose aloud in front of the class, even though I lacked confidence and was nervous. It helped that my average grade was a ninety-nine.

Back in the U.S.A. 1975

When I returned from Europe—from Gunther's in Germany, then Gerrit's in Holland—it was at the end of January in 1975. I decided to go to night college at New York Institute of Technology and take the courses I could apply in real life at The New School. I job-hunted tirelessly in the publishing industry until I landed a gig at *Vintage*, one of the leading wine magazines of the era. While it wasn't precisely a field I cared about, the fact that I got hired at a reputable magazine with a good circulation was more than I could have foreseen.

I then proceeded to find myself a cozy almost-one-bedroom apartment in a 1940s art deco building on the East Side. I moved in up the block from Katherine Hepburn, whom I'd catch hopping into a taxi from time to time.

My apartment was split in half. Half the living room window was of opaque glass block tiles, typical interior decoration of that era. It was amusing to overhear my neighbor's lovemaking noises. All I had to do was lean toward the wall and I'd be privy to oohs, aahs, and more. One time, I knocked on the wall and told them to shut up, brat that I was.

My maternal Grandpa Irving and his former nurse-turned-wife Florence enjoyed visiting my first apartment. They were so proud of me. Heck, I was proud of myself. I adored my Grandpa and Florence. Over the years, after my Grandma passed away, I'd become his confidant. Each time they'd visit, we'd go to one of my favorite hole-in-the-wall discos together, way uptown on 92nd Street and First Avenue. Grandpa would clap his hands and tap his feet to Donna Summer while I danced with Florence. Mom was a bit jealous of my relationship with her father and would nudge me to "tell me what he told you," but I didn't. I knew how to keep intimacies private. Besides, if he wanted to confide in her, he would've. He was a grown man!

Chapter 8 - I'm Gonna Be a Rock 'n' Roll Journalist

I had inherited both my parents' ability to persuade and promote. I devoted a few hours a day to making phone calls to magazines to get editors' names. Then I'd spend another couple of hours writing pitch letters on my periwinkle-colored IBM Selectric typewriter that came with a correction ball.

Before I could submit anything to *Circus* magazine, one of the most famous rock journals of its time, I needed material. The school newspaper articles I wrote wouldn't cut it. That much I knew!

During the three months I lived in Amsterdam with Gerrit, I lucked out and met Barry Hay, lead singer of Golden Earring. They were one of the most popular international Dutch bands to go gold in America. Their hit "Radar Love" went to number one on the Dutch charts and was a worldwide sensation. KISS and Aerosmith opened for the band in 1974. I wrote a review of the band's performances and submitted it to various papers in the States, to no avail.

Back in America, I spent most weekends at the hot music clubs like Max's Kansas City, CBGB, and the Mudd Club, or attending concerts at the Academy of Music. Max's Kansas City was where I felt most at home since punk and glam meshed there. To build up a decent portfolio of articles, I tasked myself with writing concert reviews of each performance I attended. My album collection had expanded to over 2,000 LPs and 45s. For each new album purchased, I'd do a thorough LP review.

The passion for collecting discs began when I was given an allowance at around eight years old. That record store in Forest Hills had headphones and private booths where you could listen to music before purchasing. Once I had my apartment in the city, I'd buy my records at the Venus record shop in the East Village while scouring the thrift store across the street for retro velvet dresses and WWII bucket cloche hats. I was a big fan of hand-beaded flapper dresses and small purses and, of course, glam fashion: glitter bell bottoms; loose geometric blouses with bell sleeves, cinched at the waist; and glittery platform shoes. Thanks to my mother's fashion sense, I was an early adopter, wearing those shoes a few years prior when they weren't quite the rage yet.

Glam rock and progressive Brit pop were my choices of top of the pops. I became a die-hard critic. It helped that I had played classical Spanish guitar since I was seven years old and had a strong musical sense. I was like a walking GPS combined with an encyclopedia (the Google of its day). I knew the whereabouts of all band members who'd left, who had switched bands, who had gone solo, who'd stayed. I listened to the likes of Emerson, Lake & Palmer, Bowie, Mott the Hoople, Lou Reed, and Brian Eno; they were amongst the faves in my collection.

One night I took the train downtown to see Roxy Music at the Academy of Music on 14th Street. It was my great fortune to sit next to G, who worked at the all-music "rock in stereo" station, WPLJ-FM, 95.5 New York. We struck up a conversation (I was prone to engaging strangers who looked eccentric), and it turned out she was also going to the concert.

She gave me a backstage pass and invited me to tag along with her; she said she'd introduce me to the band and their manager. Filled with an unbridled excitement unlike anything I had

Chapter 8 - I'm Gonna Be a Rock 'n' Roll Journalist

experienced before that moment, there was nothing I could say except an incredulous "yeah, thank you." I was trembling but didn't want it to show. I filled the blank space with more chatter as the train clanked and jolted its way to the 14th Street Union Square station.

Walking a few blocks past the unruly progressive-rock crowd, we ascended the wrought-iron steps behind the venue. We immediately gained entrance to the VIP section backstage near the dressing rooms. Groupies dressed in shredded leather punk clothing—think New York Dolls—hung around smoking weed and cigarettes; busy sound engineers, roadies, and crew members hurried around with equipment. At the same time, other hangers-on huddled around the dressing room of the band. As we approached the room, I lost the nice lady who got me here in the first place.

Then suddenly, I blanked out and fell to the ground. I'd fainted. What transpired was eerie and inexplicable. I had an OBE (out-of-body-experience) for the first time in my life. As my limp body lay on the ground, I floated about ten feet above it. I watched as a curious onlooker while people panicked and called emergency services on their ham radios. People were shocked, hovering over me, and worried if I had died. I couldn't understand why they were making such a fuss. I knew, yes, I knew inside my mind, that I had fainted and would wake up soon enough. But was it like some Victorian swooning spell? Was I too worked up, knowing I'd be face-to-face with the band?

My brain was conscious, yet my body felt as if I'd had a stroke, paralyzed inside the shell of my physique. The commotion and excessive concern on the part of everyone around the scene seemed way too dramatic, even for me. I tried speaking, then calling out, but nothing came out of my mouth. A medic arrived with a stretcher and put smelling salts to my nostrils. *BAM!* I woke up in a hurry.

The medics gently took my hand to steady my walk. One grabbed my arm and waist lending support, as Brian Ferry emerged from the dressing room, asking in his London accent, "Sorry, luvvie, are you all right now?" I would've fainted again save for the EMT guy.

After a glass of water and endless thank-yous, I went up another stairwell with G, right to the stage. I stood about fifty feet away from Brian Ferry and the fantastic Phil Manzanera on guitar. The concert began with Ferry singing "Prarie Rose" in that velvety voice of his. The rest of the show was devoted to the songs from the iconic *Roxy Music* album, their first release with jazz interludes, wild use of the synthesizer, and ballads. They ended the set with their single "Do the Strand".

After the concert, G and I headed backstage again for a few drinks and schmoozing, but I didn't imbibe much, save for the occasional beer (the various types of which I learned how to differentiate in Europe) or a glass of bubbly (thank you, France).

G and I stayed in touch and eventually she snagged an interview for me for the band that I had followed since their inception, Emerson, Lake & Palmer. They were amongst the megalith prog rock bands and had toured with Emerson's famed moog synthesizer and Palmer's incredible custom-made drum kit that looked like it came from H.R. Geiger.

Chapter 8 - I'm Gonna Be a Rock 'n' Roll Journalist

Eventually I snagged an interview with Keith Emerson who was touring with Emerson, Lake & Palmer and performing at Madison Square Garden. I got front row tickets for the show. I met up with Keith Emerson at the swanky Park Lane Hotel at four in the afternoon on a weekend.

I had a very young countenance and looked more like sixteen than eighteen. To compensate for my baby face, I put on a pair of pink-rimmed glasses, got myself a clipboard, and put that along with my recording device into a leather satchel, the kind that guys wore in Europe. I'd bought it in Belgium. Its rectangular shape snugly fit everything I needed, and the deep burgundy color matched my glasses. Off I went to the hotel. For effect, I wore my jean jacket, on which I had embroidered an armadillo from the cover of *Emerson, Lake & Palmer*'s second album *Tarkus*.

The interview went off without a hitch, and someone tried to get me to drink a few gin and tonics, which I politely refused more than once. That evening I transcribed the notes and wrote up a story.

Mind you, to this point, I had published articles on music, lifestyle, and restaurant openings in local community papers and some neighborhood rags. It was a modest beginning, but everyone needs to start somewhere. Though I didn't have the necessary credentials to make an impact, I knew it would come as long as I kept my eyes on the prize. I had fierce determination like nobody's business.

With a laser focus, I diligently submitted concert and vinyl reviews to all sorts of papers. My only goal was to establish myself as a music journalist. The ferocious dedication I gave to this pursuit cannot be understated. I didn't care if I made friends. My social life consisted of going to concerts and music industry-hosted parties, and dating older men.

As I had the knack for gab, I was able to convince record company publicists and those at the independent agencies to add me to their list of journalists who would receive press releases, LPs, updates, and other swag. Being on these lists also entitled me to attend private parties and invites to concerts, even though I hadn't yet been published in any of the well-known newspapers or magazines.

I visualized publishing stories in *Rock*, *Rave* magazine, or the *New Musical Express* of England. Never once did I doubt my abilities nor the outcome of my herculean efforts. I could taste how it would feel once my first story was in print with my name on the byline. As an A-type perfectionist, I held myself to rigorous standards. I didn't take rejection as a final no. *No* meant try again, and harder; refine my approach; and know that one day I'd see my reward. Although I felt crushed that several magazines rejected my Emerson, Lake & Palmer interview, it only made my resolve to succeed even stronger.

Finally, with unwavering persistence and chutzpah, I got a break—some traction—when *Circus* magazine agreed to publish my interview with a folk-rock artist who lived in Vermont in the middle of nowhere. It was dusk on a very blustery December; the snow was six inches deep when the publicist and I hopped on a Cessna headed to meet the artist, her client.

From that point, there was no stopping me. New York City is an unforgivingly tough market. The competition didn't faze me

Chapter 8 - I'm Gonna Be a Rock 'n' Roll Journalist

since, in reality, I competed with myself more than anyone else. Still, I needed a strategy for success to differentiate myself from the other—read: male—journalists. A majority of females worked in publicity either at record companies or in agencies. Others had secretarial jobs or, for a chosen few, marketing roles. My one good friend in the business, Lee, had been working with Michael Lang (one of the three founders of Woodstock). She was an exception to the rule. The entire world of rock 'n' roll was macho—starting with the musicians and going all the way up to the CEOs of the record labels.

Inappropriate and salacious comments and grubby touching was considered "normal." Once, I was sitting in the office of some A&R (artist and repertoire) guy pitching him about doing a promo piece for one of their new artists. In the middle of my presentation, he closed the door, sat on his desk with one leg swinging, and asked me bluntly, "Do you want to fuck me?" "No!" I retorted, "I do not." He smirked, "If you refuse, you won't get the gig—you knew that, right?" With that, I got up, cursed him under my breath just loud enough for him to hear, and slammed the door behind me.

When necessary, I fought like the tomboy I was. If I had to do combat with a bunch of dickheads to get ahead in this business, then I had no problem facing them down. It was complicated. I was a sexy young thing and flaunted my looks, yet one thing was indisputable: I would never bow so low as to go to bed with anyone in the business. Ethically and morally, I found it repugnant.

The sheer number of male journalists, freelancers, and

wannabes in the New York market forced me to think creatively to come up with that sought-after strategy: my unique value proposition. Combing through the plethora of music magazines from around the world, smack-dab in the music publishing district on 57th and 8th Avenue, I came across *Record Week of Canada* and the *Performance* - The International Talent Weekly magazine.

Eureka! A plan unfolded in my mind's eye. I would become the New York correspondent for one or both of these foreign journals. Then I could gain industry recognition, which would provide me with better access to industry happenings and musicians who were then still untouchable to me.

Chapter 9 - KISS Japan Tour 1977

Tokyo, Japan March 1977

With a few publishing credits under my belt and steadfast willfulness, I became my own agent. I'd already confronted the difficulties, personally and financially, of growing up too fast, yet my uncanny ability to persevere against all the odds and to defend my iconoclastic personality fueled my confidence. When it came to my career, I was enormously ambitious in a Leonine sense: down-to-earth practical and highly convincing, with a sense of urgency to take action. I tripped over my own feet more than once.

Everything had to happen immediately. I don't know if I thought I'd die young, but underneath my assertive, in-your-face outer layer lurked a very different person. The inner me was a dedicated daydreamer and explorer of the psychological and analytical. I used to call myself a romantic realist. Fascinated by Myers-Briggs and other behavioral personality tests, I would devise pie charts, in my imagination, as literal drawing was not my strong suit. Still, from time to time, I would indulge in pen-and-ink renditions of nature's bounty.

I split sections of my brain into parts: career, fantasy, love relationships, friends, family (the worst section), hobbies, career, spiritual life, and travel or foreign countries. I kept tabs on this "other" self through dream journals, which I began documenting after my Grandma Faye died when I was fourteen years old. I tried analyzing the dreams according to courses offered by the Association of Research and Enlightenment in Virginia Beach, which was founded by the son of the late psychic Edgar Cayce, whose theory on symbolism was a subject that piqued my interest. I often thought about light, though I couldn't explain a mathematical theory if you'd asked.

On a scale of zero to I don't know, if what I saw at zero was visible light, then what would happen after I died? Would I then be able to see the infinitesimal amount of colors blocked from my human vision and hidden from view? Was there something else that needed uncovering? Something I wasn't seeing in my own life?

On many a night, while sitting on my friend Danny's plush Italian leather sofa with a book in hand, I'd ponder that which was invisible, the future, my future. Would I be able to pay my rent? What about college? Would I be able to carry on writing if I didn't have a job? A gnawing doubt chewed away inside of me, producing an unstable and tenuous feeling.

Then Destiny came calling!

"Is this Elise Krentzel?" asked a girl who sounded about my age—eighteen.

"This is Al Ross's office, can you hold, please, for Al?" She pressed the hold button before I could respond. The Press Office was the P.R. firm for KISS, and Al managed their account. Why was he calling me?! I couldn't imagine.

I didn't like the band. Gene Simmons appeared like a bug

Chapter 9 - KISS Japan Tour 1977

from outer space on silver platform shoes several feet thick. He wasn't attractive musically or as a cartoon character. If the band's sound, look, or dance movements were sexy, I could've considered being slightly more objective in my overall review! What was it about rock music that drove teenagers mad? Sex, drugs, and rock 'n' roll. Those three magic components relayed the interdependent nature of the whole business.

"Elise," he chuckled, "I'm calling because a month from now, KISS will be touring Japan, and we'd like to invite you to be one of the KISS Army journalists on the press junket: the KISS Japan Tour 1977!

"We've chosen ten reporters to tour the major cities, including Osaka, Kyoto, Nagoya, and Fukuoka, and then top it off with four nights in Tokyo at Japan's biggest hall—Budokan—for a seventeen-day extravaganza.

"You're coming, right?" he insisted, as if he knew the answer.

"No thanks, I don't like the band in the least," I said with a snooty know-it-all attitude that only teenagers can muster, adding, "and if I can't write what I want about a group, then there's no point in my going, because what I'll write about the band won't be flattering."

He implored me to think about it and said he'd get back to me in a few days.

In the interim, I interviewed Paul Simon at a Japanese restaurant in the neighborhood where *Studio 54* used to be. Just in case I did decide to go to Japan, I wanted to familiarize myself with the cuisine. It was one of New York's four Japanese restaurants, and also my first time eating Japanese food. I learned how to effectively use Japanese chopsticks. By the end of the meal, I was gobsmacked with Japanese cooking.

Taking Broadway to walk back to my apartment, I saw the marquee for *Pacific Overtures*. I suddenly recalled seeing the Stephen Sondheim musical a year earlier. The show was a condensed *Reader's Digest* version of Japanese history, beginning in 1853 when Commodore Perry forced open Japan to the West. All I remembered about the show was its ending, where maybe fifty or more salarymen in dark suits, white shirts, and thin black ties stood onstage in military formation carrying briefcases.

When Ross's office called again, I told him I was in. He was confident I wouldn't write a negative review, and told me to just "wait and see and be ready to be shocked." KISS had recorded several albums to this point. *Dressed to Kill* had gone gold, and *Destroyer* had gone platinum in 1976. Their biggest hit before the tour was a ballad called "Beth," written and sung by drummer Peter Criss.

So it was on March 17, 1977, as soon as I stepped into the limo that came to haul me to JFK Airport, that I stepped through a portal into an alternate world. I didn't truly know what tripping on acid was like until that adventure began.

The band and their significant others, crew members, management, and the remaining out-of-state reporters met at the airport before getting on the chartered 707 Pan Am KISS Clipper. Naturally, the band boarded first.

Of all the journalists, including the renowned rock photographer Bob Gruen, there was only one other female, and she was twice my age and wrote for Reuters news service. I was the youngest at nineteen.

Chapter 9 - KISS Japan Tour 1977

The garish gals of BBQ-land (Brooklyn, Bronx, and Queens) held one or two terriers or poodles on long leashes. Their collars were festooned with gold-plated dog tags and rhinestones. How gauche! These rock wives looked like borough people even though wealth and fame could have influenced their wardrobe selection. They were bleached blondes with streaks of chestnut brown or, worse, black, sprouting through the demarcation line of part and root.

As we boarded, I overheard Rock Girlfriend One. "Oh, I don't drink O.J. in the morning—I prefer the glow of a freshly rolled joint," she said out of the side of her mouth as she chewed a wad of gum, cracking it against a molar. To me, the bleach in her hair was like the bitter taste of orange juice on an empty stomach.

Rock Wife: "Peter (Criss, the drummer) doesn't eat at all. Ya know, he could die of anorexia by drumsticks, and I don't mean chicken, doll." Such were the conversations of suburbanites gone national whose femininity was determined by the length of their fingernails.

The Pan Am Clipper had two levels, and the entire downstairs was retrofitted into first class. KISS had a makeshift dressing room built into the economy section of the plane. They were seated in the penthouse above the first-class section. As the press arrived, they didn't bother descending to greet anyone.

I lucked out. A freelance journalist from L.A. named Andrew plopped his camera and equipment down in the seat next to mine, giving me a wide, dimpled smile that was inviting yet not sexual. I don't know who was more mischievous, him or me, but we bonded like blood brothers.

He quizzed me in Japanese: "*Nihongo wakari masuka?* Do you

understand Japanese?" No, I didn't. He blurted out some more key phrases, like "*Ohaiyo gozaimasu*," meaning, "Good morning." It sounded like *Ohio-go-zay-mass*.

Responding to him warmly, I chirped, "Why not Detroit *gozaimasu* or New York *gozaimasu*?" He was in stitches.

Over the fourteen-hour flight and several plastic glasses of champagne later, we formed a pact: We'd be partners-in-crime during the tour. KISS's public relations manager took a couple of well-spent hours out of his itinerary to advise me on Japanese protocol.

He suggested that once we landed, and after introductions, I speak with Kusano-san to write a story about the tour for Japan's leading rock magazine. ("*San*" was the honorific for Mr., Mrs., and Ms. in Japan and added to a person's Christian name, he explained to me. If you are of the Hindu, Buddhist, Jewish, or Muslim faith, does one still have a Christian name? I wondered.)

Using surnames was considered impolite in Japan. Kusano-san, Al informed me, owned Shinko Music, music sub-publishers of the KISS catalog and print publishers of five major music magazines.

They also owned a production company and recording studio and had interests in TV and radio—FM Tokyo (the only FM station in Japan). They were heavy hitters for sure! I daydreamed about landing an excellent, fat freelance job with one of those magazines to write an exclusive—"Touring with KISS, an Inside Look." A first-class assignment for sure.

Al carried on teaching me about Japanese etiquette. I was a sponge for knowledge. Techniques by Al could've been a course:

Chapter 9 - KISS Japan Tour 1977

Bow low at a forty-five-degree angle. This shows respect. Procedures as follows: On one's return to an erect position, look the person straight in the eye, take the business card with both index fingers and thumbs. Study the card intently for a few seconds, just long enough to show how impressed you are with his title and position. Then bow.

Naturally, in Japan, one of the most macho cultures on earth, it will be a *he*. Do you have to bow as low if it's a woman giving you her card? I didn't know. Do women bow lower than men?

Doris, the other female on tour, yelped, "Look, there they are, fully dressed with makeup."

In unison, everyone up front turned toward KISS. Each band member smiled coyly; Gene stuck out and rolled his tongue, posing for Bob Gruen, while the others were jiving. Al hobbled to the back of the first-class section, stretched his arms and legs, and belched more instructions to the press.

"Here's what's happening, guys. Listen up. We're landing in about an hour. KISS deplanes first. They'll be escorted by bodyguards through a separate doorway. Everyone follows Rob Mistral and me through the public entrance. After clearing customs, limos branded with the KISS logo will be waiting to take you to the hotel. If anyone gets lost, just head for the exit and get into a car fast. We expect thousands of fans."

I peered out the plane's window to discover lush emerald and moss-colored hills and teeny white concrete boxes squeezed and compressed over the entire landscape. As part of Honshu Island, surrounded by the Pacific Ocean, Tokyo was a mass of industrial strength. As we made the descent, the first thing that caught my eye was a billboard on the runway with the image of an Asian Mr. Clean: bald-headed, flaring nostrils, and a gold hoop ring, pirate-style. The only difference from the American version was the eyes—black horizontal lines.

The sky was nondescript and hazy. Was that pollution? As the Pan Am Clipper edged to the left, we landed at Haneda airport, and a rush of tremendous energy seized me. There were thousands of black-haired girls bobbing in a sea of sequins. The expression *You're on* couldn't have had more clout than at the moment the plane's wheels hit the ground.

Over five thousand girls, screaming like banshees and crying "*Key-suu!*" in Japanese-English, waved blood-red, silver, white, and yellow streamers above their heads. They dressed like micro-sized KISS dolls, platform boots and all. As the plane circled the airport, one could see little girls stacked one against the other near the tarmac, on the departure visitors platform. Security guards and police forced the fans back into line with long red poles. The poles, made of a rubbery substance, bent with the force of the crowds.

Al was sweating in panic as we deplaned. Suddenly, swarms of girls broke through the red barricade and were racing to the plane. Several journalists reacted immediately, jumping to guard themselves.

"Everyone calm down, will you?" he insisted. Ever the organizer and part-time parent, he debated who was worse—the artists or the press? "Everything's under control. Let KISS walk first, and then follow me. Do not deviate or stop for anyone or anything."

Chapter 9 - KISS Japan Tour 1977

The Colonel, as Al was called, did an about-face, huffing and puffing. KISS then descended onto the tarmac to hysterical girls jumping like pogo sticks. The crowd was in a frenzy. The welcome *Key-suu* received was bigger than when the Beatles visited Japan!

Guards with bulldog features carefully cordoned off a ramp for the band, who strutted on a red crinoline carpet in full costume and makeup. They were never seen in public without makeup, in fact. The police showed no emotion as they tried to protect the group from the delirious public. The uproar was deafening. The roadies flirted, hoping to get some nooky. Some of them tossed KISS buttons and pins to the crowd.

Finally, after what seemed an eternity, management and press entourage were allowed to leave. Andrew grabbed my arm and pinched me as we ran into the parade on the red runway.

"Ouch, Andrew, not so hard," I complained. I felt myself shaking with that thrill you get right before making a public speech, even though I wasn't going onstage. All the same, I felt dizzy. Glued to my sleeve, Andrew waved to the girls, acting out his male rock star trip. More screams of delight and exhaustion. We quickly made our way into the terminal, shuffling along with jet lag. The strange loudspeaker sounds of hallowed recordings, funny accents, and wailing teenagers echoed in the din of the terminal. Above the sea of costumes, uniforms, and curious onlookers, airport signage appeared sinister.

"Wave to them one last time before saying sayonara," beckoned Andrew. He feigned sadness at leaving his groupie girlfriends standing there all alone. He blew them all a kiss. What a charmer, I thought. I liked him.

Andrew had bent down to tie his shoelace when the stampeding hordes broke loose. "Run for your life," I shouted. Al managed to save the day. He patrolled a parade of limos signaling Andrew, me, and others to hop in. Our luggage would be delivered directly to the hotel. The funny thing was that the cab doors opened and shut automatically. A metal door-type hinge operated by the driver swung the door into your shins if you weren't careful. The black Mazda was by no means a stretch. I remarked, "This is a squeezed limo."

"No, it's a squeezed lemon," said Andrew, sweating profusely.

With three to the back seat and one upfront, Randy (another journalist) was nearly sitting on Andrew's lap. It dawned on everyone that the Japanese drove on the wrong side of the road.

"Look at the doilies on the headrests—can you believe it? I haven't seen a doily since the year gimmel," I said, astonished.

"Check out the white hand-sewn gloves the driver is wearing," Andrew pointed out.

"Are we in stitches," joked Randy another journalist, "or in lace?"

"Not in your bedroom. We're in Tokyo, but if it's Tuesday, this must be Belgium," added Brian dryly. Andrew suggested that it might be time for B to invest in a compass.

Leaving the airport was tricky. Roundabouts were jammed with traffic as cars whirled by and came to short jerky stops. Huge billboards—Sony, Sanyo, Panasonic, Canon, Toyota, Mazda, Matsushita—surrounded three-quarters of the roundabout. There were puppy dog faces of sweet girls caressing small delicate electronic devices; those same pristine faces smiled, eyes squinting, behind

Chapter 9 - KISS Japan Tour 1977

the steering wheels of compact cars. The only small car I could recall seeing on the Pelham Parkway or Long Island Expressway was a VW Beetle. The limo circled the roundabout a few times until it was aligned with the other KISS vehicles, over 25 cars, as in a head-of-state procession. Little flags posted on either side of the dashboard had the KISS logo.

Apparently, the driver didn't speak a word of English. Most likely, he was told to smile and bow his head once the foreigners entered his car. That's when he switched on a prerecorded message.

"Welcome to To-key-yo," murmured a high-pitched female voice. Continuing in Berlitz-like fashion, the voice said, "*Konnichiwa* (cone-knee-chi-wa) is saying hello, and *konbanwa* (con-bon-wa) is good evening. Have a pleasant journey, and enjoy your stay in Japan."

"Must be a special service prepared for us barbaric Westerners?" I warned in mock seriousness, wagging my finger like a metronome gone berserk.

"Better learn your *a, ka, sa, ta, na, wa's*," added Andrew gaily. He began singing "Now I've learned my *a, ka, sa*" to the tune of "ABC," much to the chagrin of the other journalists, who peered at the pair of us as if we needed help.

The elevated concrete highway to Tokyo had only two lanes. It was partitioned off from the suburbs and streets below. We whizzed by smokestacks, rooftops of glass and concrete, whitewashed modern apartment buildings no taller than eight stories, and treetops on roofs. It was evident that land was a premium commodity; not an inch of it was spared. The ride was smooth until the driver passed an electronic eye.

Under My Skin

As the kilometer gauge hit 100, Andrew shifted his weight by twisting his arm around the doily-covered headrest. I was absorbing the images that raced past, but the overall impression was disappointing. My adrenaline was sky-high as I looked for sights, like pagodas, temples, anything to welcome me halfway around the world, a hint that this was Japan—even a wooden house with a tiled roof would've been acceptable. It looked as if the whole city (at least whatever I could see of it above the walled-in highway) was a jamboree of gray, white, and two-toned concrete blocks.

After descending a ramp there was a tollbooth. The driver chucked the coins in, and a little female voice recording must have said thank you, but it was drowned out by kitsch dentist office music played at 78 RPM on a triangle. *Brrriiiinnnng, brriinnng, diiiinnggg.* After the last hammering of a bell, the light turned blue. Blue lights instead of green! Also, the street lights changed color from right to left. The reshuffle meant red on the right, yellow center, and blue on the left.

Finally, we entered the Tokyo city limits. A bustling street life greeted us. Loudspeakers blasted music in public. Greengrocers and shopkeepers vied for shoppers' attention using megaphones to pitch their sales of the day. Men in conservative blue suits, white shirts, and solid-color ties walked in groups to and from office buildings like zombies. Horns honked as scooters and motorcycles zoomed by. It was far busier and ten times more crowded than the Big Apple.

"Is this the city center?" I asked wistfully to anyone listening.

"*Hai*," responded the non-English-speaking driver. "*Hai*, Tokyo *desu*," he repeated.

Chapter 9 - KISS Japan Tour 1977

My heart was beating at an increasingly fast pace. The brief wave of disappointment was canceled out by the scenes of a typical Saturday at two in the afternoon, Tokyo time.

Schoolchildren were dressed in navy blue sailor-style uniforms. Boys wore caps resembling yarmulkes, and girls wore bonnets and pleated skirts that hung woefully long below their knees. The haze gave way to sunshine, and the temperature was a pleasant sixty-seven degrees. I rolled down the window to breathe in the air. It tasted like grilled fish smoked on mesquite wood. Whiffs of roasted chestnuts entered the car.

Bob Gruen snapped photos at every turn, bend, and stop. He leaned out the front window as far as his lithe body could go and clicked in rapid succession. Schoolgirls who witnessed his action covered their mouths while giggling. They lowered their eyes in deference or embarrassment.

The mass of humanity was incredibly dense. The roads were narrow, allowing only one car access as the other lane was reserved for parked cars. Some streets had sidewalks on one side. A steep path through the city twisted and turned, up hills and on small roads with names such as *Omotesando, 246,* and *Shibuya.*

The driver pointed and called out the names, which were written in Japanese and hardly legible against bluish signs posted in no particular sequence. The chrysanthemum bouquets—white, yellow, magenta, and purple—were bulbous, sprouting from nooks in the landscaped stone gardens outside the office buildings. Bamboo trees, red magnolia, and red maples were planted in cookie-cutter formations.

"The American Embassy, *migi* (right), Okura Hotel, *hidari* (left)," said the driver, as if on cue.

"Reuters news service, *zushawi*," I said, improvising the word for *straight ahead* and pointing to the tall building ahead of us as I checked my mini-Japanese/English dictionary to see if my pronunciation for *straight* was correct. It wasn't.

The Okura Hotel, customarily frequented by diplomats and visiting heads of state, was built in a cul-de-sac in a self-contained valley. The original Okura Hotel was a Frank Lloyd Wright original, but alas, it had been demolished years earlier. The cars halted at the left-wing entrance. Bill was outside organizing.

"Press, meet in the lobby. New itineraries will be ready in twenty minutes."

He turned to greet a short, stout man who had an army of helpers around him. Kit Watanabe bowed, then cracked a huge toothy smile, hugged Bill, and the two walked off. We all congregated in the lobby, studying the Reuters ticker tape. Andrew and I roamed the hall admiring the mauve, forest green, and lilac-printed carpet and curtains. The *Playboy* magazine journalist discovered a fantastic gadget. He gestured for us ladies to come over. Scratching his head and winking, like a detective who found the last clue to the murder mystery, he declared:

"Look at this. They call it a "facsimile machine." It reproduces your text or photos at the same time you dial a phone number. You press a button, and you don't have to make a Xerox copy of your paper."

The swarm of journalists gathered around in awe as the business center's manager showed them how it worked. Speaking inaudibly, a woman regretfully informed us, "It only works in Japan and is not for international calls."

Chapter 9 - KISS Japan Tour 1977

While we were mulling around the sitting area, browsing through *Tokyo Magazine*, the English-language *Japan Times*, and the shopping guides, Kit Watanabe and Bill signaled the press to come forward.

Kit dutifully bowed to the semicircle of curious journalists and said, "*Nihon ni irashai masen*"—welcome to Japan. He shook hands with each person. His assistant, Masayoshi ("Call me Masa for a shortcut"), a thin man of average Japanese height—about five-feet-seven—with flaring nostrils and curly, shoulder-length hair, spoke with an American accent.

He handed us printed copies of the new itinerary and our respective room keys. Thank God mine was next to Andrew's. We exchanged room numbers. "Here's the updated plan," Masa blared. "Three more dates added to Nagoya. We do five nights in Tokyo, one night recording the live album *KISS Live at the Budokan*. Tour finishes on April 5, and you fly back to the States on the sixth. Any interviews you want with us, RCA Victor, the record company, or Rock Za Entertainment, you call me, 'Big boss.'" He chuckled and walked away!

I went upstairs to the sixth floor and opened the door to my room. The sound was imperceptible, as if the hinges were walking on tiptoe. The luxurious room had a king-size bed, a writing desk, a seating area for two with a table, and, in the marble bathroom, a gigantic tub. A sumptuous basket of fruit lay wrapped in cellophane. I couldn't make out what the orange, tomato-shaped fruit was. Ah, a persimmon, I discovered in one juicy bite. Mangoes, pineapples, and what appeared to be an apple covered in kiwi-colored skin (guava), and a prickly-looking cactus were beautifully arranged. The card attached read, *Elise Krentzel, Journalist, Welcome to Tokyo.*

I had never slept in a five-star hotel, but the interview I did with Keith Emerson at the fancy-schmancy Park Avenue Hotel a few years earlier was not as elegant as this. I definitely hadn't seen an all-marble bathroom with a phone hanging from the wall. I found a cotton summer kimono of blue and white with bell-shaped designs. It was folded in dry cleaner's plastic on top of the counter of the double sink. Red, scented glycerin soaps were packaged in octagonal boxes finished off with red ribbons. A pair of terrycloth slippers was tucked under the sink.

It's gorgeous, I thought. So well appointed, sophisticated, and subdued.

Andrew phoned me about a half-hour later. "Hello, yeah, it's me, Andrew. Did you get a load of the baskets of fruit? What about the kimonos and slippers? I'm definitely using that sash to wrap a little Japanese girl in my arms," he exalted.

"We'd better plan our own itinerary for tonight away from the rest of the press— don't you think that's in order?" I inquired.

"If I don't see anyone's face or talk with any of the others, believe me, it's no skin off my nose," Andrew concurred.

We set a time to plan something devious, before the scheduled dinner at 8:00 with Bill Aucoin. Bill was KISS's brilliant manager who discovered the band at a small club. He kept to himself on the flight over to Japan and spoke only to the band and their partners, not to any of the journalists. I don't know how he did it, but Andrew had secretly arranged for the three of us to meet for dinner at the hotel's four-star French restaurant.

Opening the sliding glass onto the terrace in my room, I stepped out and took a slow breath of early spring air. Faint music. A flute's notes lingered in the distance. Below, I spotted

Chapter 9 - KISS Japan Tour 1977

the first Shinto temple I had ever seen in my life. Cobblestone steps led in jagged procession to a small wooden structure resting on pedestals with a flared, slated roof. I made out a jumble of red and white attached to the branches of the Formosa trees nearby and thanked God for this unbelievable good fortune. I promised myself to write a great review of KISS, despite earlier misgivings. How could I not? I was grateful for this opportunity.

I changed into a red slinky Diane von Furstenberg wrap dress with the waist-length button-down caramel-colored leather jacket with a real fox fur collar that my Mom had given me. That's one of the main ways she showed her love: through gifts of clothing and Hallmark cards for birthdays and holidays. After a luxurious bath, I met Andrew in the Polynesian bar. It was already six-thirty. There were few patrons that evening.

"Here's the game plan. Since tomorrow's our free day, what I want to do is go to the downtown section and check out the bars. There are hundreds of these holes-in-the-wall in the Roppongi district. It's known for nightclubs and foreigner hangouts. We'll slip into one of the funny office buildings about so high." He described the width and height visually, using his hands—the left making an L and the right forming a number 7. "And walk in or out of any place we choose."

Enchanted, my wide eyes showed it. My unruly head of permed hair bobbed up and down as I blinked a few times in recognition. Nothing I wouldn't do on a typical night out in Manhattan—barhopping, clubbing. Why not?

"Maybe I'll even bump into some of my old cronies—Americans and Brits who teach English—and we can bum around with them," Andrew said.

"I overheard Masa mention an ancient village—it starts with an *A*—in Tokyo. Asakusa, I think? He recommended we see it tomorrow during the day. He also said there was a Shinto shrine that survived the bombing during WWII as well as a performance of geisha girls, a kind of reenactment of nineteenth-century call girls," I enthused.

"Did you take along a guide book—a *Frommer's* or *Insight Guide* to get some background info?" he asked.

"No, but I'm sure the hotel concierge or that guy Hiroo we met with Masa can direct us. And what about you, stupid? You've been here before. What am I worried about? Nothin'," I said, feigning a Brooklyn accent. After our drinks, we headed up to the restaurant to meet Bill.

The elegant room was done in faux Beaux Arts with stained-glass chandeliers. Tiffany or copies, I wondered? Plush velvet Louis XIV chairs with thick lion heads on the feet of the front legs stood at attention. Murals of peach, gold, and forest green hung on the walls. Gold carpeting as smooth as an eiderdown was laid in the center of the room. The maître d' wore a white blazer, buttoned up to his Adam's apple, adorned with a red rose. The front- and back-room staff was scurrying about. They all bowed when their gaze met ours.

"We'll have a bottle of Cristal champagne to start, and after we've finished, you can replace it with another, until I say, 'stop,'" Bill said, beaming with delight. The waiter bowed and slid away.

"I can see what type of night this is going to be," I mused. "It's three glasses tops for me, then finito; otherwise, I'll never wake up tomorrow." I couldn't take too much champagne; it made me queasy and gave me headaches.

Chapter 9 - KISS Japan Tour 1977

Bill lit a cigar and inhaled with gusto. Twitching his nose, he was bursting with the good news. "KISS will be interviewed at the Budokan before the night of the live recording by NHK-TV. Did you know that's the equivalent of the BBC in Japan? They have over sixty million viewers.

"A gold record in Japan sells one hundred thousand copies compared with the U.S.'s one million. And KISS's last two LPs went gold within one month of release here." We nodded as more champagne filled our flutes.

He continued nonstop, "Besides the U.S., Japan is the biggest market for the band. Didn't you see those kids at the airport? They're mad for the group here. Kit Watanabe and Honda over at RCA Victor say it's because their exaggerated clothing and makeup strikes a chord of resemblance in this nation weaned on Kabuki and Noh theater. They're more like puppets than a normal rock band." He blew out a circle of smoke. I coughed.

"I know what Kabuki is," I chimed in, "'cause I saw a Broadway show last year, *Pacific Overtures*. But what's Noh?"

"Kabuki can drag on for hours, and it's full of color, Noh is its opposite. It's like a dance in slow motion. The costumes are blasé, usually brown or gray robes—monk's robes. Masks are worn. Each mask represents an emotional type or archetype—the devil, the master, the philosopher, the village crazy, or the pretty maiden. The stories are oral traditions acted out as was done for over a thousand years." Bill joyfully passed on his acquired knowledge.

He let us in on another secret. In Osaka, we would visit the all-female revue, Takarazuka. This was one-hundred-eighty degrees in contrast to Kabuki. Meaning, the females are butch lesbians as opposed to the homosexual male Kabuki performers.

"Sounds exciting," commented Bill, raising one eyebrow toward Andrew.

It also sounded exciting to *moi*, as I hadn't quite figured out if I was genuinely bisexual. As a lifestyle, that is. My attitude was, "I'll try anything once, except hard drugs."

On our third round, I glanced at the menu and decided upon coquilles St. Jacques gratin as an entrée, as it was something I had never tried or heard of.

Andrew got down to business. "So, Bill, now tell us what's really behind this total extravagance. Why did you spend ten thousand dollars per head?" Quickly calculating out loud, he continued, "That's ninety thousand for the journalists alone, another twenty-five grand for the plane—okay, a quarter mill on this tour? What's so damned important about KISS?"

"Fact is, this is the last hurrah for the band. After the Pacific tour and Canada, we record one more album, and then the band's finished. We gotta get the most mileage out of sales here for next year. 'Course, you both knew that," he said condescendingly. Then he quickly added, "The press never liked KISS from the start; they always got terrible reviews, and still do. No matter—fans love 'em around the world. What's more important?" he asked acerbically.

"Yes, but then why did Al invite certain persons—no names mentioned—who you know will write negatively about the tour?" I asked provokingly.

"Because bad press is better than no press at all. Circulation figures..."

Chapter 9 - KISS Japan Tour 1977

Well past midnight, the polite staff reminded us it was time to close. We reluctantly drained our champagne glasses, then said good night as the waiters bowed us out the door.

Chapter 10 -
A Night With the Yakuza

Kyoto, Japan **March 1977**

We arose for an early breakfast and ate quickly. There was a choice of either Western breakfast or Japanese. I chose Japanese: pickled radish, miso soup, rice, grilled fish, probably mackerel, and some salad. No one wanted to miss the first day's foray to the ancient district that survived the bombs during WWII. Entering the subway station, we watched dumbstruck as platform patrol officers, called "crammers," pushed people into the cars. They squeezed them in sardine-style, every unnecessary cell being sweated out of their bodies.

No wonder the Japanese are all fat-free, I mused. Unintentional aerobic exercise is provided by the Japan National Railways promptly at 8:00 a.m. Waiting on the platform for the next car, I tried to avoid the onslaught of humanity. Did I look like Gumby? The pushing procedure was initiated. Soon hundreds of feet were stomping on mine, his, hers, everyone's. Not one woman wore tennis shoes to work as women in NYC so smartly did. I was wearing ballet-style flats, and they got ruined.

Arriving in one piece at the vast Shinto shrine in Asakusa-Ku (a *Ku* is a district or arrondissement), which had a gigantic metal bell, we witnessed people praying over huge pits filled with burning incense. They clapped their hands three times then bowed.

Little pop-up shops sold trinkets on the road leading to the muted and age-chipped, red brick-colored Shinto shrine poles.

I avoided two of the New York journalists—one, Chris, whose cynical attitude was a sad cousin of benevolence. I thought he needed the motherly love he didn't get growing up. I could relate to him on some level since I didn't have love as a child, but it didn't change the fact that I loathed him.

I had learned to cover my hurt with bold and extravagant gestures. Or humor. Anything to push away the agony. When I felt criticized, I'd strike without remorse, using cutting words to slice through my pain. But of course, that would engender more trouble. I'd resort to crying only when I was alone.

Then there was Brian. He was utterly contemptuous and a gossip columnist to boot, and he hated women. He most likely fucked his way to the top to get in the good graces of industry elites. I guess he would've spread his legs for any man! Unlike me, *ahem, ahem*, the self-righteous, finger-wagging moralist! Read: sarcasm.

Contradictions aside, one thing I vowed *never* to do at the outset of my career was to bed down with anyone in the business. It was just wrong for me, and besides, I was adamantly dead set against females who used their gender and sexuality to get to the top. I disdained them for not using their brains, skills, and expertise. It would be a lazy excuse for a *Ms. Magazine* reader, Gloria Steinem, and Jane Fonda feminist like me.

I witnessed how my father went from being a passive role model to a petty dictator with meltdowns if his inane directives were not followed. That convinced me to stay away from certain types of male authority figures and to not cave in to their demands.

Chapter 10 - A Night With the Yakuza

By lunchtime, Andrew and I had stumbled into a noodle shop, having split off from the group. Oh well, we didn't give two shits. To our astonishment, and probably theirs, the male customers slurping soup stopped to stare at us *gaijin* (foreigners) in disbelief. Loud, guttural noises emanated from deep within their steamy bowls.

After we finished off our ramen and Kirin beers, I asked anyone who listened to direct us back to the Hotel Okura. Andrew had no idea how to get back—let alone the name of the subway stop. But no one understood us. In a gesture of goodwill, the owner scurried around the counter, directing us to the street. He jabbed his finger frantically at a landmark that we couldn't make out. I thanked him with a mediocre bow and was left to my own devices on the sidewalk. Eventually, we made it back to the hotel.

Japan was a magical kingdom steeped in tradition, but none that I recognized. I was familiar with some Jewish customs and holidays, and Russian-East European culinary traditions learned from my grandparents. I didn't even know much about WASP American folklore, because what I read in the history books I knew to be a falsified version of the truth. Besides Thanksgiving or Christmas (or at least the gross commercialization of the latter holiday that America had made), I couldn't name one.

Generally I disdained tradition and equated it with tyranny. I'd preferably have been labeled a heretic for not following any, since authority, which I respected on the one hand, was also a source of oppression. I didn't want my soul, mind, or body to be smothered by any outside elements. I'd had enough of that growing up.

Over the first week of our seventeen-day tour, we boarded the Japanese *Shinkansen* several times and flew via ANA airlines—to Osaka first, and then onward to Kyoto and Nagoya in the southern part of Honshu Island, and then Fukuoka, and back again to Tokyo on April 1st for the historic four-night run at the Budokan.

The band traveled by limousine to avoid the hordes of teenage girls who were sure to cause mayhem in every city. The "bullet train" was an engineering feat unseen anywhere else in the world. It sped along like a rocket ship at no less than one hundred thirty miles per hour. Not being mechanically inclined, I couldn't wrap my head around why the train felt like it wasn't moving. Nor could I figure out how our to-go sushi lunch boxes didn't fly up in the air on hairpin curves.

After the first night's dress rehearsal (one of many we would be privy to throughout the tour) and sound check, our motley crew met at a *robatayaki* restaurant. Everyone was there: all the Japanese music industry heavy hitters and their staff, KISS, their partners, the roadies, crew, and us journalists.

Skewers of meat, vegetables, and seafood were placed on rectangular-shaped firepots, gingerly glazed, and rotated until thoroughly cooked. The chef took the finished robatayaki and delivered it on a wood peel to the customers. Japanese cuisine was extraordinarily diverse in cooking methodology, with an exquisite variety of fish and vegetables.

Kusano-san sat next to me at dinner. He relished the glamour of the music business. His company was the leading music publishing company and owned the sub-publishing rights for the

Chapter 10 - A Night With the Yakuza

entire KISS catalog in the territory of Japan. His company also represented the Elvis Presley music catalog (among other artists), so The King lived on in the mind and heart of this Japanese multimillionaire. I dug some C&W music, and I wanted him to know that.

Music publishers were responsible for getting record deals (RCA Victor for KISS) and convincing promoters to book concert gigs. Kusano-san, an exuberant character, liked being on the scene with the stars. A big fan of Nashville, he reminisced about his visits to the Grand Ole Opry, how he wore a 10-gallon hat there and back home in Tokyo and ate real beef at a dude ranch. His best memories of America were all set in the South.

When he talked to this New Yorker, he was speaking to a foreigner, an outsider. What did I know about the South? The only place I'd been to south of the Mason-Dixon line was Miami Beach—the so-called Jew Coast! My impressions of Southerners were stereotypical: drawling, Confederate flag-bearing, angry *I'm-out-to-get-you-boy* sheriffs who drove Chevys and followed New York license plates in hopes of a brawl or fistfight!

I avoided discussion of my political leanings, so Kusano-san didn't catch wind of my malady: a severe case of anti-Americanism. He thought most Americans were hospitable, friendly, open, and inviting. That was a fair assessment! But there were nuances and grave differences amongst people, geographical location, and ethnicities.

Rock Za, the best-selling rock music magazine in Japan (equivalent to *Circus* back home), was also owned by Kusano. Kusano-san was sitting to my right, and the editor-in-chief of *Rock-Za*,

Maki-san, flanked me on my left. I remembered Al's advice to ask them about writing a diary on the road. I didn't want to miss such an opportunity. So after downing too many bottles of sake to count, I offered them the exclusive insider look at life with KISS on the road. They both bowed their heads (in place of a handshake) to signal the green light. I had to deliver the story by the end of the first night in Tokyo.

Maki's offer for the story was higher than *Record Week*'s. I was high on cloud nine and rice wine. Geez, how would I get up the next day? Even though I wasn't consciously aware of how my own intuition worked, I knew, like Andrew did, that I would stay in Japan after the tour ended. The neurons in my brain told my heart it was the right thing to do—the best possible outcome.

I phoned Maki-san at the *Rock-Za* office the next day to plant some seeds about the idea of my staying on in Japan after the tour. She promised to speak with Kusano-san.

Several days later, the KISS Army (that is, the journalists on this press junket and all other staff) found itself in the ancient and magnificent temple city of Kyoto. Formerly the capital of Japan, the name is an anagram of Tokyo. After another wildly successful KISS concert with tens of thousands of screaming fans dressed up as the band, Andrew and I decided to let loose in the "old town."

Dazzled by the stream of neon in every imaginable color, we walked through the nightlife district's bars and *mizu shobai* establishments, mesmerized. *Mizu-shobai* means "water trade"— the vulgar term for any precarious form of business yielding an income entirely dependent on the patronage of its customers,

Chapter 10 - A Night With the Yakuza

such as entertainment provided by geisha, bars, cabarets, and so on. Even the music industry was considered *mizu-shobai*.

On each passing block were wedged concrete, glass, and wooden houses with four-story-high individual neon signs competing for attention from would-be customers. The crowds were impenetrable—human traffic jams obstructing passage in all directions. Impervious to others, we shoved our way through tiny openings. The pachinko parlors' *bing, bing, bing* sounds were heard in the background. Japanese punk rockers with green-and-orange-tinted Mohawks rode Honda motorcycles through the main road, revving their engines. The *mizu-shobai* located at street level employed rough men who shouted like circus auctioneers, "*Irashai, irashai, koko desu*" (welcome, welcome in here) to passersby.

Stepping into a narrow entrance, I suggested, "Why don't we enter this pink-painted building with gold neon?" Into a tiny lift—capacity one and a half humans—we both went.

"I notice this is not an Otis," I jested. "What do you think B_1 stands for?" I pressed it and, without waiting for Andrew's response, said, "I think this must be a clinic or something medical. Look—*B_1, B_2, B_3*. It's where you line up for vitamins."

Andrew shook his head as we got off the elevator. If he were from New York, he would have said, "*Oy vey, oy gevalt.*" Instead, he said, "Let's go into that one," and pointed down a dimly lit hallway. We sauntered into a club just as a door—covered in pink leather like an upholstered couch turned sideways—opened. Two hefty men stood on either side of the entrance. They sniffed invisibly for hidden weapons or contraband. One gave Andrew a fiendish look to jolt even the most diabolical club doorman in Brooklyn.

"What do you think is the matter with them?" Andrew shivered.

I could feel his goose pimples. "Leave it to me. I'll find out what's going on here," I said. I walked right up to the shorter of the two, who was a tad taller than me, and without compunction, requested directions to the cloakroom. He waved to his colleague to take our jackets. Snapping his fingers suddenly, four boys appeared. They couldn't have been older than twenty-one. They greeted me first, then Andrew.

Taking me by the arm, they seated us in a booth nearest the dance floor. A globular silver disco ball hung, glittering through the lights as a live band did cover songs—from Sinatra's "My Way" to the Beatles' "And I Love Her."

"This is so kitsch, isn't it?" I rasped above the music, pointing to the interior. Little did we realize the roles are reversed in some Tokyo nightclubs. Before Andrew could answer, two boys knelt beneath my feet. One poured me a whiskey while the other daintily took ice from the bucket, asking in Japanese, "One ice or more?" I didn't drink whiskey and asked Andrew to change the order. He tried translating that, but to no avail, so he bungled his order for Coke on the rocks. Two other boys delivered a Coke and rum without ice.

"What do you think these boys are doing here?" Andrew asked, but he couldn't hear me over the sound. Leaning toward him as he squirmed between the long-limbed pretty boys who surrounded me, I became suspicious.

"I feel uncomfortable. I know we don't belong here. It looks

Chapter 10 - A Night With the Yakuza

like a pickup joint for women who choose and then buy young boys. Look there," he said, pointing to an old lady dancing.

"Stay put, let's see what's going on. Don't be such a bore!" I implored, but I, too, was getting nervous.

The woman's wrinkled face suggested wealth. Her diamonds and emeralds confirmed it. Wearing a kimono, she portrayed a retiring figure dressed in humility. Until she sat down. Out of the corner of my sharp eye, I saw the woman drag the boy's hand to her breast and insert it, Napoleon-style, inside her kimono. She cooed and mussed his hair as he coyly mixed her another drink while obeying Madame.

One boy settled his hand on my stockinged leg while stirring my drink. I tried telling him, unsuccessfully, that no, no, I didn't want his service. He sat patiently, hand on my leg, awaiting my next instruction. Apparently, *no* was not in the Japanese language, or it wasn't permitted at this establishment.

"I'm afraid we better leave. This is, no pun intended, getting out of hand. See?" I pointed at the limp hand clamped like a car lock on my leg. Using the international sign language for the check, I scribbled the bill midair, gesticulating to one of the waiters.

Immediately a bill for over three thousand yen was presented in an expensive leather pouch. Two wrapped mints were the bonus for payment. Except that we couldn't possibly pay the outrageous bill. Horrified, I did a quick mental calculation.

"Andrew," I said, gulping visibly, "this glass would cost us the equivalent of one-hundred-plus U.S. dollars."

Wait, wait—I had to count all the shot glasses to tally the

amount. We had, what, one, two... I started counting the glasses. Andrew had two, I had two. Good, together that made four hundred dollars. Neither of us had thought of exchanging additional money for that evening. Desperate for a solution, I waved over the bully, who immediately came over with his bulky frame and scowl, his hand out—wanting cash only!

"Mr.... I mean, San...no *nihongo*. Do you speak English, Mr. San...." He filled in his name, Satoru, angrily. "Yes, Mr. Satoru—manager-san *desu ka?*"

Andrew sat, still allowing me to carry out this fantasy alone. Mr. Satoru tagged behind the manager who was cleanly shaven, wearing a black tuxedo and white tie. I half expected him to wear the obligatory white gloves I had seen on the taxi driver from the airport. I bowed. The manager stood aggressively with his legs wide apart in an A-shape with his arms crossed. He repeatedly pointed to his nose, indicating that he indeed was the manager.

"Mr. Manager-san. We have a small problem here. In my country, America..." I had no plan, so I improvised in the moment, coming up with an ad hoc response to this dilemma. Craftily, with one hand on my hip, I told him that I charge much, much more than three thousand yen. "Ask my manager here, Andrew-san," I said, pointing to where he was in the booth.

I beckoned Andrew to stand and bow, to be on the ball to corroborate this ludicrous story. He moseyed over to me and stood slightly to my right to listen. The club manager looked pitifully at Andrew but was keen to know more about my nightly rates, wink-wink. Unperturbed by his questions, I continued with the charade.

Chapter 10 - A Night With the Yakuza

"Therefore, Mr. Manager-san, I'm afraid that since my charge in America is six thousand yen," I said, inclining my head in Andrew's direction and nodding vehemently, "we will have to charge you three thousand yen for my presence here tonight."

He inquired as to the specific service I was to deliver.

"If you want to know that, you will have to visit me at my hotel tonight at 3:00 a.m. But first, you will have to pay me half—one thousand five hundred yen. Here." I jabbed an index finger in the middle of my outstretched palm. "In cash. You can hand it to my manager in an envelope."

I scribbled a fake hotel name on the back of Manager-san's business card and lied about my name. Pregnant pause. Some discussion between Manager-san and Satoru. Dirty looks toward Andrew. Pretentious smiles in my direction. Bowing. Agreement.

Manager-san was on the brink of making a counteroffer when he took me by the elbow toward the pink door. He showed me the outstanding bill. I shrugged, tempting him to try me. Finally, he gave in.

"I give you three thousand, you pay no bill, and I see you later in the hotel. You do what I say in hotel. I pay you no more yen. OK?" He was satisfied.

There was nothing humane about the man. He looked like a cold-blooded murderer. The pinkie of his left hand was chopped off—a telltale sign, I was to learn, of membership in the Japanese Mafia known as the *Yakuza*. I bowed in acceptance of the offer and went to kiss him on the cheek. He moved away. Satoru slipped an envelope to Andrew.

We escaped down the stairs. In the stairwell, we gaped at the cash. Andrew was astonished at my chutzpah and at the money! I was frustrated that Andrew hadn't even offered to intervene. But the cash was real. The thugs fell for the story.

Andrew and I had enough cash to party for five more days, but not in a host club. I counted the one-hundred notes and handed Andrew a cool thousand and a half. Split evenly down the middle.

After much cavorting, we returned to the hotel, exhausted. With a cavalier attitude, Andrew sauntered down the hall, flapping his yen notes in the air. Twenty minutes later, just as I was about to cuddle up in the quilt, there was an explosive banging on my door. I immediately shot out of bed and saw Manager-san through the peephole. As I undid the lock, he roared into my room. He was maniacal.

Yelling in what sounded like gargling words in Japanese, he stomped toward me. I rightly assumed he wanted his cash returned. And then some! The door was ajar, and I screamed. Just as he leaped for my throat, Hiroo from RCA Victor, on guard duty that evening in the fourth-floor hallway, flung himself heroically on the manager. Everywhere we went, either the record company or Udo Artists—the concert promoters—had security guards who protected every floor of the hotels we stayed at. The men now rolled on the carpet.

Andrew heard the pandemonium. Startled, he ran out into the hall in his *happi* coat (Japanese cotton kimono) and peered into the room. Lifting both arms up tentatively, Andrew raised his shoulders and eyebrows. What could he do? What should he do? I cocooned myself in a nook. After much skirmishing, yelling,

Chapter 10 - A Night With the Yakuza

and cursing, Hiroo and the manager untangled themselves and stood up. The manager rapidly shot words like a boxer throwing jabs.

Hiroo asked me to explain the story as he spoke spitfire into his CB radio. He had called Masa, who was staying in the same hotel that evening. Hiroo thought it a good idea for Masa to be present to report the story to Kit Watanabe himself. Andrew gingerly stepped into the room and voluntarily aided me by offering his arm as support. His mere presence consoled me.

Masa arrived alert and expectant. "I wish I could curse in Japanese right now," I said to Andrew. "If I could disappear and become invisible, I would snap my fingers and, *poof,* be gone."

"Stand up, Elise," ordered Masa, "and tell us exactly what happened here and why Manager and Hiroo are in this room." He dismissed Andrew with a bark and told him to wait outside the door.

I took a deep breath then apologized before the inquisition committee.

"We entered this club tonight and didn't realize it was a host club for women, you see. So like two ordinary people, we sat down at a table and ordered some drinks. There were young boys, four of them, in fact, who came by and sat with us. After one or two sips of the liquor, I asked for the bill because somehow I got the impression the club was private or somewhat unique. I didn't want to run up more charges.

"Unfortunately, my instincts were right. The bill was hundreds of dollars more than what we originally thought because we didn't calculate any other charges like entry fee, extra person fees. Thinking on my feet, I challenged the manager—to see how far he'd go. I made up some story about how I charged much more in the States for my sexual services and suggested that he pay me, which he did.

"We then arranged to meet this evening at my hotel. I wrote out a false hotel name and faked my name, thinking he'd never find us in this city of fifteen million, with thousands of hotels and tourists."

Masa made me, and then Andrew, apologize with deep bows and loud "sorries," loud enough for the night staff at the hotel to blush in embarrassment. (Japanese feel that way because the group is more important than the individual, and if someone in a group does something so embarrassing as to compromise their honor, then those around seem to feel the shame.) Then we returned all the money we stole from Manager-san. Since there was an outstanding bill for over eight hundred dollars that we chalked up at the bar, Masa paid it to Manager-san, as we had neither that kind of cash with us nor credit cards.

As a punishment, Andrew and I were curfewed for the remainder of the tour. We had to stay with the group and report our every movement and plans. We were not allowed to go out on our own. The following day I heard the Pat Benatar lyrics in my head, "We are young, heartache to heartache..."

How could Andrew and I have been so bold, outrageous? A goof in the lives of two in Kyoto. My gift for improvisation should have been applied to acting, not journalism. The ease with which I came up with that crackpot story to the *Yakuza* middleweight was downright dangerous. We could've gotten ourselves thrown out

Chapter 10 - A Night With the Yakuza

of the country with a "Re-entry not allowed" stamp in our passports, kicked off the tour, or worse, murdered. Killed by crew-cut men without necks. Yucko! Disembowelment by swords, *seppuku* by force. Thanks to Hiroo and Kit Watanabe, who saved us, we're alive today. Alive in living color.

Chapter 11 - Trouble in Paradise

Nagoya, Japan 1977

About a week later, a group of us ventured into an outdoor flea market during our free time. As Andrew would tell me later, he paced briskly to catch up with Brian, who was far ahead of the others. He was trying to figure out how he could extract information regarding a rumor he'd heard that Brian had written something nasty and highly unsubstantiated about me. Panting, he asked Brian if he'd been up to anything daring.

"I heard a rumor that you wrote a not-so-nice story about Elise. Is that true?"

Brian skirted the issue. "I got the first interview of the trip with Gene. Nothing extraordinary, nothing I don't already know. It's sent. Out. Filed. Doris was edging for the interview for Reuters, but we'll be the first with the scoop!" Brian boasted.

"What scoop?" prodded Andrew. As far as he knew, there was none.

"Didn't you know? Can't you see it with your own eyes?" asked Brian quizzically. "Elise. She's faking her credentials. She's a groupie. No one has even heard of *Record Week* or *Music Express*—have you?" He waited impatiently for Andrew's answer.

"Sure. I know both those rags. They're well known on the West Coast. The magazine's HQ is in Vancouver, which, by the way, is also on the West Coast." Brian ignored him and pressed on. The lipstick, the red dress, high heels...he laid out his "facts" while rolling his eyes for Andrew to see.

"She was invited by Gene as one of his plaster casters. For variety, when he got tired of the little Japanese."

"Can you prove it?" Andrew asked flatly.

"Proof? There's proof enough! She ingratiated herself to Al on the plane, and then with the band. She ate dinner with Bill alone, *and*," he emphasized, "before she went upstairs yesterday, I overheard her plans with Gene and Paul. Meetings were set with each one separately for tonight, Gene at eight and Paul at ten, alone, secluded, in their rooms." He huffed with scorn at Andrew, who, in his opinion, couldn't possibly tell fact from fiction. "Rest assured, Andrew, you'll see it for yourself..." He trailed off, adding triumphantly, "or read it in next week's column."

Andrew didn't like being the bearer of bad news, especially as he had a soft spot (and a hard-on) for me. He felt it was his duty as a reporter to inform me a storm was on the way.

As Andrew would later describe to me, anger had swelled in his chest at the thought of Brian's petty selfishness. He couldn't see why Brian wanted to deliberately destroy me (in Andrew's eyes, a girl first and journalist second) and my reputation. To Andrew, Brian was a small-minded nerd. Besides, the entire story was based on conjecture. Andrew had a vision of himself as a big brother. Perhaps I would then, with tears falling from my innocent eyes, rest my head on his masculine shoulder for support.

Andrew watched me rummage through antique dishes and teapots in the marketplace. Slowly approaching, he rested

Chapter 11 - Trouble in Paradise

his arm around my neck. "I've got some really horrible news to report." My nostrils flared, and panic clumped in my throat as I braced myself. I had a peculiar ability to detect a person's emotional essence. "Brian wrote in his column that you are Gene's groupie, and that's your claim to fame on this tour."

Tears swelled in my eyes, and I moaned in silence. "So fragile emotionally, so rock 'n' roll robust externally," Andrew said gently. Then he attempted a joke. "Things could be worse...for example, it could be true." Before I regained complete composure, he ventured, "Is it true?"

"It's baseless!" I shot back aggressively. "Sticks and stones will break my bones...but tonight I'll string him up by his balls. He can't face me, did you notice? Not a word since I met him in Manhattan. He's afraid of me. I'll show him that his fears are well grounded." I gave Andrew a caustic smile, indicating Brian's days were numbered. Then I dashed around the nearest corner and wept in private. Andrew came after me to console me and get me back to the hotel.

Banging on the door of Brian's room that night, I insisted he open up. When I had phoned earlier requesting a brief meeting, he had hung up on me. Ten minutes later, my wrist was aching from banging on his door, but I persisted.

Brian sulkily flung open the door, then let me inside and flopped on the sofa. He did not offer me a seat. It was up to me to explain why I requested his time. He nonchalantly waited to hear what this "groupie" had to say to him, the oh-so-important on-the-scene-columnist he imagined himself to be. Hovering above him while keeping an eye on his hands, I started calmly.

"I heard what you wrote about me." He fiddled with a spoon. His lips were taut. No comment.

"I want to see the article. *Now.*" I raised my voice a few decibels. He didn't budge. "If you don't show me that article, I'll search for it myself."

I began digging through his papers on the writing desk, tossing books, magazines, and loose scraps of paper in all directions, as I repeated the question "Where is it?" louder and louder as if speaking English to a foreigner. I'd had enough.

He jumped up, displaying his weak muscles by grabbing me by the shoulders. I swung instinctively and bashed him in the face. He was stunned.

"Don't cover your face, you clueless prick!" I grabbed him and squeezed his crotch so hard, noticing he had hardly any balls to speak of. He shrieked and shrank to the floor, writhing in agony. "If you had any balls at all, if you would've questioned me about *Record Week,* if you would have investigated the paper, you would've known about me. But no...what does Mr. Know-It-All weakling gossip columnist do?"

I answered my own question, "He writes bullshit and lies!" I screamed.

Like a mother about to punish her child, I waited for his cry-wolf story. Brian's left cheek was cherry red, his receding hair disheveled. With groin in hand, he sarcastically informed me, "It's too late. The article's gone. I'll give you a copy next Monday so you can proofread it."

He smirked at me, relishing my lack of self-control. He was superior in every way, disgusted that a person like me could be

Chapter 11 - Trouble in Paradise

on the same tour as him. Outwardly cold and quick with words as I was, I was no match for him. In an uncontrollable rage, I spat on the floor and stormed out of his room, slamming the door on the way out.

Obviously, the commotion stirred some people and raised some eyebrows amongst the super-polite hotel staff. Andrew came into my room, scrutinizing my red knuckles.

"You didn't do what I think you did, did you?" he ventured. I revealed my prowess and strength by demonstrating to him my performance—jabs, slaps, and punches, waving my arms. Andrew was laughing as I mimicked my outrage. "Congratulations. Great performance. Think we can ask Gene if he needs an extra onstage?" he teased.

"What I'd rather do, since I can't control the outcome of the article, which he already sent by Telex, is go out tonight with you and party." I resigned myself to this reality, offering him a mopey grimace. Nothing could be done. He concurred.

"Brian said you had an interview with Gene and Paul tonight. That's not true?"

"Not at all. I scheduled it for next week in Fukuoka, before the Takarazuka show. Why do you ask?"

"Because he overheard you making plans." He gave me the "facts" as he had heard them.

I ignored him. How fatuous, I thought, but at the same time, I had a need to confide in Andrew. I couldn't contain myself.

"I'm absolutely bewildered at my own violence, Andrew. I don't know what got into me. I couldn't stop myself. I wanted to hurt him, really. The last time I hit someone was my mother. I was fourteen. She was about to slap me when I grabbed her by the wrists. I looked her in the eyes and warned, 'If you ever lift a hand to me again, I'll lift mine back.'

"From that time on, she never did." I pondered. "And the time before that was eons ago, at Girl Scout camp, when someone tried to steal my s'mores off the campfire."

My reputation was at stake. I felt as if I'd been stabbed in the gut. "Let's just get ready and hit some bars," I said, changing the subject to recover. Andrew nodded, clapped me on the back to cheer me up, and grinned his famous dimpled grin. He looked perplexed; I could tell he was mulling over the frustration he obviously knew I was suppressing.

"I don't think I've ever met anyone like you, Elise! How are you so fiercely autonomous, yet incurably vulnerable?" He then proceeded to offer some advice straight out of Psychology 101. I rolled my eyes to heaven.

"Elise, maybe you're too serious about life. You're too passionate, too sensitive. You should learn to let people be. Ignore them. What do you care if someone doesn't approve of you, or if they write something mean? You've got to let go. Roll with the punches."

"C'mon let's get outta here, I'm hungry." I grabbed his arm, and we ventured out.

Chapter 12 - Bigger Than the Beatles

Tokyo, Japan April 1977

During the final week of the KISS Japan Tour 1977, while back in Tokyo, I crammed in some more interviews with the band members. The first one was with Gene a couple of hours before the biggie at the Tokyo Budokan, which was being recorded live for an upcoming album. He was in full make-up and regalia—the tongue-thrusting vampire figure, ready and hyped-up for that afternoon and night's live recordings. They were doubling up on April 2, 1977, for a live release that would shoot them up the charts to number one in Japan and worldwide. That was the plan, anyway!

Before I could utter a question, he pulled out a pile of over one hundred Polaroid photos of women he called "plaster casters." Showing off in a most unattractive and misogynistic manner, he rolled off the names of the women he had screwed in undulating delight.

"Look here, it's Cher," as he flipped through the pile.

"Nice, Gene," I commented, not amused, without a shred of warmth in my voice. "That's not why I'm interviewing you. Tell me something about the tour or Japan, something that impressed you."

He laid the photos on the coffee table faceup so I could look at Cher's boobs, which held zero interest for me. "Absolutely everything. The fans mostly, because we didn't have to promote our schtick. They got it immediately and viewed us as superheroes, like in a comic book. They understood the theatrics and the magic of our music. That's why we brought the set with us, to dominate their imaginations."

The set he spoke of was a massive, million-dollar-plus-worth of equipment.

"Did you ever burn your mouth when you breathe fire?" I inquired.

"A practiced trick of the trade it is," he smirked, without revealing a thing.

Their stage presentation was undisputedly one of the most popular in the world: blood spitting, fire breathing, and other visuals. Our twenty-five-minute interview was nearing an end. Before I departed, Gene yelled out, "I'm a star, a larger-than-life hero." Yeah, Gene, you are. I nodded while rolling my eyes.

After that most boring of interviews was over—for heaven's sake, egoists are indisputably thick-headed, I thought—I headed up to my room and bumped into my buddy Andrew in the hallway. He suggested we have an early Kirin beer before the afternoon concert as we were expected to be at both shows, afternoon and evening.

I spent the following morning and half the afternoon writing the article that would appear in *Record Week, Canada*. Always super organized, after each interview I transcribed in longhand the cassette tape recording onto my legal pad so it was all ready to be typed up and submitted. Since I was overseas and had a tight deadline, I had to Telex the story from the hotel lobby. That

Chapter 12 - Bigger Than the Beatles

took well over one and a half hours since there were all these start, stop, pause, go back symbols I had to learn to ensure the script had little or no typos or errors. By the time I was done, the sun was setting.

The cover story was printed on May 16, 1977, in Record Week *under my pseudonym, Elise Lorraine.*

The KISS Tapes in Japan

Nothing in the world could have brought me more thrills than traveling on the first-class Pan Am "KISS Clipper" 747 to Tokyo. Just imagine 27 people, virtual strangers, meeting on a plane, knowing the trip about to commence would take fourteen hours, not aware that after crossing the international date line they would witness phenomena beyond their wildest dreams—well, at least I thought so. KISS would not only revolutionize the Japanese populace's expectation of a rock concert, but also gain the respect that only a few groups have ever achieved in the Land of the Rising Sun.

KISS might have been the first men on the moon for all the press they got in Europe and America and for the history they would make in Japan.

The band grappled with a different kind of superstardom in the imperial country. With all the talk about Klaatu and everyone comparing that minor Canadian band to the Beatles, I compared

Under My Skin

KISS's *popularity* to the Beatles', not their *sound*. Japanese fans and promotion people at the record company agreed, as KISS had reached top ten status on the Japanese charts more than once. KISS's second live album, *Alive II*, recorded in Japan, was a huge success internationally.

KISS and the Beatles are the only groups ever to have sold out Tokyo's Budokan four nights in a row. KISS also brought with them the largest onstage set and entourage ever to tour Japan (and Canada and the U.K. to follow). KISS is so gigantic that no one can touch them. Yet they're pretty down-to-earth guys, so regular and normal. If you are around that magic for a short while, you get a glimpse of how they make the switch from street dudes to superstars. The contrast from everyday clothes to highly intricate costumes and seven-inch platform boots; from a rugged look to heavily made-up Kabuki-like cosmetics and hair treatments; from jokesters to monsters is handled so professionally and with such ease that it's hard to think of them without their KISS cover.

Bigger Than the Beatles

Their magic precedes them. In concert they could be Frankensteins, Tigers, Mothras—sinister, adorable, hypnotic, or all of the above. Gene's favorite actor growing up was Lon Chaney. I could see how he could go from watching the original black-and-white silent *Phantom of the Opera* to creating the fire-eating, manga-like character in KISS. It made sense that Ace and Peter Criss were more popular heartthrobs than Gene and Paul in Japan. Perhaps because they are shy? Peter shed light on the situation:

Chapter 12 - Bigger Than the Beatles

"In Japan, the girl fans like each one of us individually, unlike in America, where they take the band as a whole. That's probably why Ace and I are more popular here. They can see we are not the same sex symbols that Gene and Paul are."

"KISS are the four elements, just as the Beatles were, but KISS are larger than life. The most important people to them are their fans, and we could care less about the press. Our fans make us come alive," Ace Frehley said. "From the very beginning we paid for our own publicity and promotion campaign. We invested in ourselves, and without that, we wouldn't have been able to travel this far."

Gene emphatically adds, "An object, person, or thing that is imposing, and KISS are, always leaves a second question in your mind. Our fans are unpretentious, they want loud rock 'n' roll, they want a beautiful show! No longer do kids have to look on the other side of the fence to see if the grass is greener."

Bill Aucoin was the genius behind KISS's early success. He invested in them before they ever signed with Casablanca Records and understood the value in their stage makeup and that their outrageous costumes would be successful globally. He predicted correctly that KISS would be bigger than the Beatles.

I sympathized with the Japanese, who had waited so long for their favorite group to perform. This tour was beyond monumental! The beginning and the end of it was the sole purpose of playing Japan. All that really counted to KISS and to me was the last four shows at the Budokan, which sold out eleven thousand seats. The Budokan is more than a concert hall. It's not Madison Square Garden or a football stadium. It's completely unique in structure and symbolism. It represents thousands of Japanese lives that change each time they enter the hall. It was built for sumo wrestling. Yet transformed into a concert venue—when you see thousands of non-English-speaking people stand up and scream alongside the band, "I want to rock and roll all night and party every day"—elicited in me a sense of universal connectivity to every last person standing there. Sort of like when one holds hands with strangers in a group and feels the electricity of human exchange. I had a similar reaction to seeing the Broadway plays of *Hair* and *Jesus Christ Superstar*. That type of togetherness brings a greater purpose to living, a sense of achievement of something greater than your own little success story.

Eddie Kramer flew in from New York to produce and mix the live album. Kramer, a legend himself from South Africa, was one of the most sought-after recording producers and engineers in the business. He has collaborated with several artists, including the Beatles, David Bowie, Eric Clapton, Jimi Hendrix, the Kinks, KISS, Led Zeppelin, the Rolling Stones, and others in the Rock 'n' Roll Hall of Fame. KISS will be the only group besides the Beatles ever to release a live album recorded in Japan while pulling it off by selling over a million copies.

At the beginning of KISS's Japanese concerts, a DJ comes out and shouts in English, "KISS—the hardest-working band in the land!" Then, like clockwork, the audience screams and flips out. Truly, they live up to their reputation as hard workers who bust their chops. They deserve all they receive. Japan was the one place where *thank you* meant much more than just a figure of speech. It was said with a true feeling of gratitude.

Chapter 12 - Bigger Than the Beatles

I thanked Al silently. He's the publicity manager who invited me on this tour. Silly as it may sound, simply experiencing the oneness with the Japanese audience made the trip worthwhile for me. I also felt a deep connection with the country and a sense of camaraderie, a familiarity with the Japanese in a way I never had in any of the nine European countries I had visited a few years ago.

I wasn't sure if KISS would scare the audience after they settled back down in their seats. I imagined them to be like puppets blasting out their 4/4 beats. The audience expected the exact opposite! They wanted KISS to spit out multicolors and Ace to fly. They wanted Peter to prance and kill like a feral cat and Gene to kiss them. Gene was a master marketer and knew in advance how they'd react: "We are innately human, but we do things that aren't, thinking you are not supposed to like showing guts."

"There's a gory fascination that the Japanese will love, because we display certain things that are similar to Kabuki theater and *hara kiri*—the act of dramatic suicide. With KISS, it's impossible to sit at a show, so don't expect that."

Gene did not take four days, five hours, and six seconds to decide that when he joined KISS, he ought to be a monster character. It was a part of him, a somewhat suppressed part that made more sense to reveal onstage than through killing someone or while walking the streets of Queens. Gene isn't as weird as some make him out to be. He's not into the occult; rather, he's level-headed and analytical about the business of KISS.

"When I was a kid, Lon Chaney was my idol," he waxes on. "Ever since I was a kid, I was fascinated by the way he could change his face and image. He distorted and deformed himself into something that scared people, that made them speculate. He was larger than life, and I wanted to be that way too."

In some ways, Simmons couldn't accept the fact that he was human and had to perform human functions. He wanted to transform himself into a "wild flying thing." "I'm still intrigued by the power of unknown beings and things. I love science fiction and thriller movies and could probably name every actor, producer, and director dating back to the 1930s," he boasts.

His act onstage was by no means accidental. Simmons was taking fire-breathing lessons way before he ever thought of being in a band. He was a schoolteacher and watched monster movies that employed the arts of deception. I wondered how that came off to his students, but he wouldn't say.

After the show, when I spoke with Ace about his impressions thus far, he said, "They respect us more than rock 'n' roll because it's a disciplined country that breeds respect toward their elders and those they admire. That's the status quo, unlike in the States, where people are so prejudiced about little things. Like here, it's more of a foursome, while each one has their own fans, but the fans look at us as one unit. That's not the same in the States."

Peter Criss's crooning song "Beth" made all the girls scream and cry. He put it this way: "I love attention. A drummer is always in the background, makin' noise. He never gets out there in the spotlight. I sing four songs and save "Beth" till the end so the momentum and sexuality is stronger. This is also the first time we've used our new set, and whether the Japanese realize it or not, they are seeing KISS at a special high point."

Chapter 12 - Bigger Than the Beatles

"The girls love Ace and I more over here for some reason, possibly because we are not as outward onstage as Gene and Paul." Paul was keeping a low profile during the tour, as he missed his girlfriend back home. He admitted, "It's hard, ya know, touring nonstop for three years. Usually I run around, but I don't want to go out every night; I need to rest up." That coming from the sex bomb of the group.

I noticed there were hardly any boys or men in the audience. Ace smirked at my remark, adding, "That's because Paul Stanley is a sex symbol, as are some of the other members, like me."

KISS are regular guys from the borough of Queens, in New York City. Proving my point, one day on tour we visited a Buddhist shrine in historical Kyoto, the former ancient capital of Japan, with its hundreds of temples. KISS allowed strangers to take photos of them and even held some of the children in their arms. Can you name a band that has time for that sort of thing? Politicians do it, but most rock bands are caught up in their superstardom.

On the one hand they may be regular, but according to their road manager, Billy Miller, "Usually in other bands there is a camaraderie between one or two of the guys that goes beyond the band. They may hang out together and get into each other's personal lives. KISS go their own separate ways. They're four different points: north, south, east, and west. It works for them, and there's not much bickering among the members. From the time they set foot on that stage, they are completely professional—which is more than I can say for your average rock band today."

Billy knows, as he worked for Jerry Weintraub for many

years. By the time he was 27, he had road-managed Sinatra, Elvis, John Denver, Eric Clapton, the Rolling Stones, Moody Blues, and a host of others he says he can't remember.

I caught up with Paul to talk about the band's professionalism and down-to-earth approach. Paul insisted, "Our makeup is not a costume. It's really us, because we bring KISS wherever we go. We're still common people, and we never lose sight of ourselves. We relate to what we're doing. In fact, the most powerful thing to see is someone who can handle power. Every member in the band keeps each other in check. I need someone to mirror my actions."

Yet being on the road for years on end has to take its toll, and as Paul admitted earlier, puts wear-and-tear on intimate relationships. He confided, "I'm very old-fashioned. I'd like to have a one-to-one relationship. There's no love on the road; there's lust. A deep, meaningful relationship cannot take place in the course of a few hours. Sex on the road is dynamite. If you spend your time searching, it can stare you in the face and you wouldn't know you were in love. I figure if I work hard, sex might as well live up to my expectations. Bad sex is the worst thing, but good sex is unbeatable and hard to find. I'm romantic and sentimental."

The tune he wrote while in Japan, "Love Cup," would appear on the next album. I wasn't privy to hearing it in advance, so I couldn't decipher whether it was romantic and sentimental like "Beth" or not.

The songs performed in order:

"Detroit Rock City"

"Take Me"

Chapter 12 - Bigger Than the Beatles

"Let Me Go, Rock 'n' Roll"
"Ladies' Room"
"Firehouse"
"Makin' Love"
"I Want You"
"Cold Gin"
Ace's Solo
"Do You Love Me?"
"Nothin' to Lose"
Gene's Solo
"God of Thunder"
Peter's Solo
"Rock and Roll All Nite"
"Shout It Out Loud"
"Beth"
"Black Diamond"

The roaring applause did not subside for a good fifteen minutes after the band walked off stage. The audience lit their lighters to produce thousands of flickering points in space. In unison they swayed as if the wave of light would roll like the ocean reaching the band backstage to bring them automatically back.

Then for one last time in April of 1977, KISS appeared onstage at the Budokan and threw bouquets of flowers to the audience, who screeched and cried.

Chapter 13 - Landing the Deal

Tokyo, Japan April 1977

The KISS Japan Tour 1977 was headed back to America a day after the final concert, but I stayed on a few days longer—enough time for me to take Kusano-san up on an offer to meet him and the editor of *Rock Za* in person at their HQ in Chiyoda-ku, wherever the hell that was!

Al was not pleased with my declaration of staying on in Japan, but I assured him that the article was going to be printed in May and he'd get a copy as soon as it was published. We said our farewells and that was that. I only cared about telling Andrew of my decision to linger a few days since he, too, was planning on staying in Japan. He had fallen for a girl and was off to be with her. Andrew had relatives in Tokyo. He phoned them and they allowed me to spend the extra two nights with them until my flight back to New York.

The next day I was off to meet Kusano-san at Shinko Music. Don't ask how I found my way there, what with getting lost earlier in the tour, not being able to read any of the signs, and not understanding the color-coded subway map. However, I did arrive on time for my appointment.

I walked into an open office system totally uncommon in the States. Each section, and there were many, had two rows of adjacent desks facing one another, with one placed perpendicular to them at the head of the rows, forming a *T*. I learned that each section was a department, and the *T* desk was reserved for the head of the department. Interesting!

During the meeting I learned that Kusano's empire, called Shinko Music, included music publishing divisions, domestic and foreign, that published several music magazines, including rock, jazz, and folk, and was also the largest importer of all kinds of books and publications from three major printed music publishers: the world-renowned Hal Leonard Corporation, Music Sales Limited, and Warner Bros. Publications.

Shinko also boasted artist-management services, studio recording, concert engagements, record label placements, and master recordings for the artists signed to the company. The firm represented thousands of titles in a variety of categories of sheet music, band scores, songbooks, folios, and artist biographies. I was impressed with Shoo (the nickname Kusano encouraged me to use) and with his massive company. What I liked about him was his easy, familiar way of speaking, unlike the formality of many Japanese, who appeared rigid. He seemed to have an innate understanding of American egalitarianism while still commanding the respect of his peers and juniors.

After much polite talk, introductions to all the department heads, and too much green tea, Shoo asked me if I would like to work together. I wasn't about to pass up this offer, no matter what it entailed. As I had intuited earlier on the tour, when we met at dinner, I felt I had some connection with Shoo and also Japan. He told me, "I think you'd be a great 'mascot' for the company. I'd like you to land us more sub-publishing deals with artist management in the U.K. and U.S.A."

Chapter 13 - Landing the Deal

It sounded thrilling. "What would that take?" I queried.

"You'd help us find the right musicians and their managers, and we'd buy the foreign rights of their music catalogs for Japan."

I had plenty of ideas and was eager to impress him. "You mean, like, from bands you haven't yet heard of?"

"*Hai, hai!*" Shoo and the entire management team nodded their heads in agreement while grunting.

For that, they needed a front person, someone with charm, street smarts, and knowledge of the inner workings of the music industry. Even if I didn't know everything about the industry, I was a hustler and could meet anyone, so long as I was focused and determined. I was ahead of the curve when it came to up-and-coming talent as I had my finger on the pulse of the industry, especially with Brit alt bands, punk, and hip-hop, and so was the perfect "mascot" for the job. I accepted. Kusano promised to send me a one-year contract, a round-trip ticket, coverage for the cost of shipping my clothes and other personal effects, and an apartment, so that when I arrived in Tokyo, I would be able to move right in.

I returned stateside and informed my family that I had landed a plum contract in Japan and that I'd be moving for at least one year. The family members with whom I was still on speaking terms were thrilled for me. I wasn't talking with my Dad again, since he disapproved of my going to Japan in the first place. All he wanted was for me to become a secretary and get married, and I was having none of that bullshit. I informed my roommate that I'd be leaving in July, which gave him enough time to find someone else or move out of the spacious digs on West End Avenue.

Under My Skin

I packed a few boxes, and by June, my belongings were in a container headed east for Tokyo. On July 1st, I bid farewell to my mother, stepfather, brother, grandfather, and his wife, Florence, and best friend Miche, hugging and crying at the Pan Am terminal at JFK. And so it came to be: Twelve hours after take-off, I was officially living in Japan. I looked forward to celebrating my twentieth birthday that summer with new friends and colleagues, excited to begin an entirely new and foreign chapter of my life.

Epilogue - The Bamboozler

Tokyo, Japan & NYC 1984

Who would have thought the way I'd almost leave Japan was on a bike? Let alone on a bamboo bicycle encrusted with gold-leaf handrails and hand-painted jade green mudguards that took the shape of bamboo leaves on a golden bamboo frame?

It was a typical hot, sultry Tokyo summer night. Monsoon storms descended on the concrete jungle in sweaty swaths. Steam was everywhere, dripping off everyone. The only place at night for some R&R was the coolest disco in Roppongi, Wheels. The air conditioning was sublime; waitstaff scooted to the psychedelic patterned tables on roller skates delivering cocktails— yet another got-to-keep-up-with-the latest-American-trend happening in Japan at the end of 1983. In the swirl and boom-boom of Duran Duran, Pet Shop Boys, and Prince, two light-haired, very tall foreigners appeared to swagger onto the dance floor under a fanatic glitter ball throwing prisms on the frenzied crowd.

They scoped me out, another round-eyed devil, as if my electric blue orbs were part of a club whose X-rays were visible only to *gaijin* (foreigners). Without any introduction, bemused, and not a little tipsy, the taller of the pair (who later revealed himself as Fritz) dragged over his friend Johan and tempted me onto the dance floor, straining at the same time to make small talk, which was impossible. The waiters whizzed past while he brayed in an unrecognizable tongue. I coyly demurred and flung myself in Johan's direction, making an "oy vey" face, rolling my eyes to heaven, pointing to Fritz the Ditz. Johan reminded me of a wolf. His grayish-brown whiskers and eyebrows shaped like upside-down Vs suggested magician. He danced like a very unenlightened whirling dervish, swinging and hitting people helter-skelter with his limbs.

We were like two magnets whose fields drew us straight into each other. Amazingly, though, he didn't bump into me. We floated in tandem poetically, and that felt just great. Even though I was seriously dating Yujiro at the time—a refined young man for whom I felt the utmost respect and tenderness (he imported European antiques and spoke English and French fluently)—this weirdo German got the girl jumping.

In the desperate irresponsibility of the moment, Johan and I were making out on the dance floor, rolling on our backs, providing the crowd a delightful exhibition of lust. No one seemed to care; they continued dancing around us. Johan's English was moderately good for a German; his Japanese, nonexistent. Nearly closing the place at 4:00 a.m., we trod up the hill to the notorious pink *kisetan* (coffee shop) at Roppongi's main crossroads and left Fritz to make his way home. After downing a few coffees and some doughnuts, bleary-eyed, we managed to set another date to meet later in the week.

The two Germans had been in Tokyo for three months,

Epilogue - The Bamboozler

looking for investors or producers for an invention of Johan's, to no avail. They had a blueprint of a bicycle they hoped to manufacture and some venture capital that got them over the ocean to the Land of the Rising Sun, but not a cent more.

"How in the world did you guys come up with such a faulty plan, without a plan B?" I grumbled. They had no contacts whatsoever! What kind of entrepreneurs were these two backwater yodelers? I figured the initial investor must have had some ties to Japan, or else why would he throw away his money? They all assumed Tokyo was the prime spot to develop an idea the whole world was waiting for: the Bamboo Bicycle.

Once they showed me the blueprint of their grandiose design and outlined their marketing plan for the States, I became intrigued (whereas earlier I'd thought they were just idiots). The risk they took was absurd: In case they couldn't find an additional investor, then what? They'd be stuck in Japan without a pot to piss in. Here's the rub: I was so terribly judgmental of others, yet when I would do something equally stupid, it was fine. That's because I believed in my superpower to defy physics.

When I believed in something, I almost certainly got it. When it came to relationships with men, though, I was codependent and emotionally pliable. A colossal conflict waged war inside of me: a fiercely independent spirit vis-à-vis a desperate need to please. That's why I settled for men who loved me less than I was worth and refused the ones who loved me more than I thought I deserved. This was something I didn't know how to resolve until much later in life. But the Bamboo Bicycle—that I could handle. I tossed Yujiro and what-could-have-been to the wayside.

Johan was the artist/visionary and creator of the product. Fritz acted as Johan's manager and salesman, detailing the level of craftsmanship they desired, explaining how the product was to be positioned, and outlining an opportunity for me to take control of manufacturing and production. For my part, they offered thirty percent of sales after expenses, which they would cover. After some deliberation, I reconsidered and offered up a proposition.

I made sure to get something in writing. Even though I was idealistic, I instinctively knew that, without a contract, if things went south, it would be my word against theirs, and I'd probably lose, since I had no clue about international laws.

There was no way I could have known that their so-called company in Germany was nothing but a front, even though I had this piece of paper with their signatures on it. Sure, I could have phoned the number listed on their business card, and then what? The investor didn't work at their company.

I trusted two total strangers because I was ever the thrill seeker. To get involved meant putting my faith in myself. I knew I could produce the vehicle in Japan and promote it in stores in the U.S.A., and that I had the advantage over Fritz, who definitely could not. I believed I could rack up commissions in the thousands after I sold the bike in the imagined future. Taking on the challenge to prove I could do it was an unwise business move, to say the least. There were also Johan's sexual intentions with me, which helped the gifted duo fiddle me like a violin.

The entire concept was outlandish enough to appeal to my peculiar tastes. My business life was as unpredictable as a roller

Epilogue - The Bamboozler

coaster, dependent upon outside forces and the whims of the market. While I continued freelancing, I was involved in projects that were either huge successes or miserable failures—no middle road on my horizon. The more abstract a concept, the more practical I became in getting it off the ground, running, and profitable. I applied an earthiness to future outcomes and excelled in situations where I could produce an end product—something concrete from thin air, a vision of beauty, a sense of the unusual, an original form. Though I felt at home working in the arts, I had less than amicable feelings toward some of the whiny, spoiled artists.

Until then, my experience was limited to musicians, those in the music industry, and some artists. The former were egocentric and not too intelligent (compared with pop musicians; jazz musicians were in another class, in my stratified hierarchy) and the artists possessed lame, destructive tendencies, resulting in abusive behavior and total mistrust of anyone else.

The Bamboo Bicycle was to be marketed as an upscale toy for the rich and famous, aimed at the ladies who lunched. And we couldn't forget those power-breakfast boys, born with Daddy's silver spoon in their mouths, who invariably shopped at Brooks Brothers for their suits and were members of the New York Athletic Club. This was the perfect item for them to drop an easy four hundred bucks on.

At my insistence, Fritz wheedled more desperately needed funds from the investor in his hometown of Hamburg, Germany. Until the money arrived via the American Express office, the two of them were holed up in a dingy room in Tokyo without windows, sleeping on moldering futon mats. There was no hot water in the flat, which meant they had to take showers and baths at the public *onsen* (Japanese bath house). They had only a Bunsen burner for a stove, and a W.C. that looked as if it had come from the other side of Alice's looking glass.

Despite their miserable living conditions (and my intuition that alerted me to walk away as quickly as possible), my insatiable ego took over, telling me to produce the damn thing. So that's what I did.

Because a rebellious heart knows how to defy gravity.

I researched factories that could produce the bicycle to the standards Johan envisioned. Johan came along with the horse-and-pony show, flashing his marvelous blueprint and hare-brained scheme of fame and fortune while I translated. We eventually found a mom-and-pop firm located 45 minutes outside of Tokyo's megalopolis that could perfect the manufacturing, molding, and hand-painting needed for one prototype. A few months later, the Bamboo Bicycle was ready to be revealed to the world. The precious cargo was sent ahead by boat and the three of us flew to NYC a few weeks later. We stayed at the Empire Hotel. Within two weeks of arrival, I landed purchase orders from the upper echelon retailers: Bendel's, Saks, and Hammacher Schlemmer.

I proudly delivered the order sheets to the boys at the hotel, waving them like a freedom flag. Out of the blue, Fritz had a seismic meltdown. I'd never confronted someone with a psychotic disorder in my entire life. I thought I'd seen it all when it came to wackiness, but a violent reaction of such magnitude I had not.

Epilogue - The Bamboozler

Compared with Fritz, my mother's fits looked like child's play. I was scared out of my wits! He went about slashing the furniture with a knife, throwing silverware and bottles around the room. Then he took a steak knife from the turn-of-the-century American-style cherrywood room service table and flung it in the direction I was running: the corner of the room where the Bamboo Bicycle was parked.

"Johan, help me!" I screamed. Johan ran forward to protect me and the precious cargo. God forbid the bike should get a scratch!

The knife landed on the carpet, luckily, but not before I tripped over a bottle. Continually screaming his lungs out and rampaging, sickly Fritz admonished me while jumping around the suite, "You sold out! No one told you to sell out!"

"Sold out? What are you talking about, you raving lunatic? I sold the bike. I made us sales, you jerk. I didn't sell you, or Johan, or me out, I sold the thing we're in New York for...or did you suddenly forget that's why we're here?"

Fritz's twisted face was sweaty and red hot. He pulled open his damp shirt, revealing a white undershirt as if to show some, what, muscle? Some Tarzan-like chest full of hair, when there were actually just a few blond limp strands? I was disgusted. Johan jumped from the corner and grabbed Fritz by the shirt collar, then pushed him onto the bed in a chokehold.

"He's got an illness, Elise. He's schizophrenic."

"You're crazy too," I screamed. "Both of you motherfuckers are demented."

Tending to him like a baby, Johan rubbed Fritz's forehead

and patted his hair with a towel. Eventually, the adrenaline crash knocked him out and the mad salesman fell into a deep sleep.

Maybe it was me who sold out myself? I grabbed the bicycle and fled while Johan was in the bathroom. Even with 24 speeds, that bike couldn't have gotten me out of the hotel quick enough. Department stores never saw the Bamboo Bicycle. I rode it to safety and never encountered those two crazy guys again.

Acknowledgments

First and foremost I want to thank the various editors who worked with me on this project: Deb Ewing for her ability to grasp nuanced meaning and put it in place and time, and Marli Higa whose insightful copyediting pulled the whole book together.

Kudos to my cheerleading team who from start to finish egged me on, while challenging me to do better. My son Florian Krentzel, Taylor Goodwin, and my beloved (deceased) friend Wendy Nolin who spent hours listening to me read, moan and brainstorm ideas. Thank you to graphic designer Stefan Silvestri of Gebr. Silvestri, (and Marvin Fernandes), who brought to life the essence of *that* girl whose story is told here.

www.elisekrentzel.com
www.instagram.com/elisekrentzel
www.facebook.com/officiallyelise

About the Author

Under My Skin is Elise Krentzel's first novel and part of a trilogy. She was formerly the Tokyo Bureau Chief of Billboard Magazine, the first foreign DJ at FM Tokyo and introduced punk rock music to Japan. Elise founded the first digital travel guides with GPS pre-internet, blogged before it was a "thing", ran a non-profit in South Africa to combat AIDS in teens. She is a ghostwriter of non-fiction books. She mentors adults who have grown up in dysfunctional families. Elise has one son and lives wherever she finds herself.

www.ingramcontent.com/pod-product-compliance
Lightning Source LLC
Chambersburg PA
CBHW072155200426
43209CB00052B/1264